23 pt **TYPOGRAPHY23**

LIBRARY
FRANKLIN PIERCE COLLEGE
RINDGE, NH 03461

LIBRARY
FRANKLIN PIERCE COLLEGE
RINDGE, NH 03461

1 pt THE ANNUAL OF THE TYPE DIRECTORS CLUB . . . .

2 pt THE ANNUAL OF THE TYPE DIRECTORS CLUB . . . .

3 pt THE ANNUAL OF THE TYPE DIRECTORS CLUB . . . .

4 pt THE ANNUAL OF THE TYPE DIRECTORS CLUB . . . .

5 pt THE ANNUAL OF THE TYPE DIRECTORS CLUB . . . .

6 pt THE ANNUAL OF THE TYPE DIRECTORS CLUB . . . .

7 pt THE ANNUAL OF THE TYPE DIRECTORS CLUB . . . .

8 pt THE ANNUAL OF THE TYPE DIRECTORS CLUB . . . .

9 pt THE ANNUAL OF THE TYPE DIRECTORS CLUB . . . .

10 pt THE ANNUAL OF THE TYPE DIRECTORS CLUB . . . .

11 pt THE ANNUAL OF THE TYPE DIRECTORS CLUB . . . .

12 pt THE ANNUAL OF THE TYPE DIRECTORS CLUB . . . .

13 pt THE ANNUAL OF THE TYPE DIRECTORS CLUB . . . .

14 pt THE ANNUAL OF THE TYPE DIRECTORS CLUB . . . .

15 pt THE ANNUAL OF THE TYPE DIRECTORS CLUB . . . .

16 pt THE ANNUAL OF THE TYPE DIRECTORS CLUB . . . .

17 pt THE ANNUAL OF THE TYPE DIRECTORS CLUB . . . .

18 pt THE ANNUAL OF THE TYPE DIRECTORS CLUB . . . . . .

19 pt THE ANNUAL OF THE TYPE DIRECTORS CLUB

20 pt THE ANNUAL OF THE TYPE DIRECTORS CLUB

21 pt THE ANNUAL OF THE TYPE DIRECTORS CLUB

22 pt THE ANNUAL OF THE TYPE DIRECTORS CLUB

23 pt THE ANNUAL OF THE TYPE DIRECTORS CLUB

Copyright©2002 by the TYPE DIRECTORS CLUB 0101011101110111000011111000101110101110111101010111110001111110001011110001011110111

```
01011 <html>
01010 <head>
11010 <title>Acknowledgments</title>
01000 <meta http-equiv="Content-Type" content="text/html; charset=iso-8859-1">
01100 </head>
00100
00011 <body bgcolor="#FFFFFF">
10010 <p>TDC48<br>
01010 ----------------<br>
11010 THE TYPE DIRECTORS CLUB GRATEFULLY ACKNOWLEDGES<br>
10101 THE FOLLOWING FOR THEIR SUPPORT AND CONTRIBUTIONS<br>
01110 TO THE SUCCESS OF TDC48 AND TDC2 2002:<br>
11100 ----------------<br>
00001 DESIGN: DESIGN MW<br>
01000 EDITING: SUSAN E. DAVIS<br>
10001 ----------------<br>
00101 JUDGING FACILITIES: SCHOOL OF VISUAL ARTS<br>
00111 EXHIBITION FACILITIES: THE 2 WEST 13 STREET GALLERY / PARSONS SCHOOL OF DESIGN<br>
10101 CHAIRPERSONS' AND JUDGES' ILLUSTRATIONS: ANISA SUTHAYALAI<br>
10101 ----------------<br>
00110 TDC48 COMPETITION (CALL FOR ENTRIES):<br>
00001 DESIGN: DESIGN MW<br>
01010 PRINTER: UVX LITHOGRAPHY BY LITHOGRAPHIX, INC., / LOS ANGELES / CA<br>
00000 PAPER: MOHAWK PAPER MILLS<br>
00000 PHOTO: GENTL & HYERS<br>
00010 ----------------<br>
00100 TDC2 2002 COMPETITION (CALL FOR ENTRIES):<br>
10010 DESIGN: GARY MUNCH<br>
01010 PRINTER: INTEGRATED IMAGING CENTER<br>
01110 PAPER: SAPPI FINE PAPER<br>
01110 ----------------<br>
11100 THE PRINCIPAL TYPEFACE USED IN THE COMPOSITION<br>
00001 OF TYPOGRAPHY23 IS<br>
01000 AKZIDENZ-GROTESK<br>
10001 ----------------<br>
01001 FIRST PUBLISHED in 2002 BY<br>
11010 HBI, AN IMPRINT OF HARPERCOLLINS PUBLISHERS, INC.<br>
10111 10 EAST 53RD STREET NEW YORK NY 10022-5299<br>
11010 ----------------<br>
01010 DISTRIBUTED IN THE U.S. AND CANADA BY<br>
10101 WATSON-GUPTILL PUBLICATIONS<br>
01111 PHONE (800-451-1741) OR (732-363-4511) IN NJ, AK, HI, FAX (732-363-0338)<br>
10100 770 BROADWAY NEW YORK NY 10003-9595<br>
11001 ISBN (0-8230-5558-2)<br>
11110 ----------------<br>
00101 DISTRIBUTED THROUGHOUT<br>
00111 THE REST OF THE WORLD BY<br>
10101 HARPERCOLLINS INTERNATIONAL<br>
00000 10 EAST 53RD STREET<br>
10101 NEW YORK NY 10022-5299<br>
11010 FAX (212-207-7654)<br>
11101 ISBN (0-06-008148-1)<br>
00001 ----------------<br>
11000 THE LIBRARY OF CONGRESS HAS CATALOGED<br>
10111 THIS SERIAL TITLE AS FOLLOWS:<br>
10101 TYPOGRAPHY [TYPE DIRECTORS CLUB (U.S.)]<br>
00100 TYPOGRAPHY: THE ANNUAL OF THE TYPE DIRECTOS CLUB.-/-<br>
10101 NEW YORK: HBI<br>
01011 2002-ANNUAL.<br>
10010 ----------------<br>
10110 TYPOGRAPHY (NEW YORK NY)<br>
00010 1 PRINTING / PRACTICAL - PERIODICALS.<br>
00011 2 GRAPHIC ARTS - PERIODICALS.<br>
10001 1 TYPE DIRECTORS CLUB (U.S.)<br>
10000 ----------------<br>
00100 ALL RIGHTS RESERVED<br>
10111 NO PART OF THIS PUBLICATION MAY BE REPRODUCED<br>
11100 OR USED IN ANY FORM OR BY ANY MEANS -<br>
11001 GRAPHIC / ELECTRONIC / OR MECHANICAL /<br>
10111 INCLUDING PHOTOCOPYING / RECORDING / TAPING /<br>
11100 OR INFORMATION STORAGE AND RETRIEVAL SYSTEMS -<br>
00000 WITHOUT WRITTEN PERMISSION OF THE PUBLISHER.<br>
01000 ----------------<br>
10001 PRINTED IN Hong Kong<br>
01011 ----------------</p>
10010
10111 </body>
00010 </html>
```

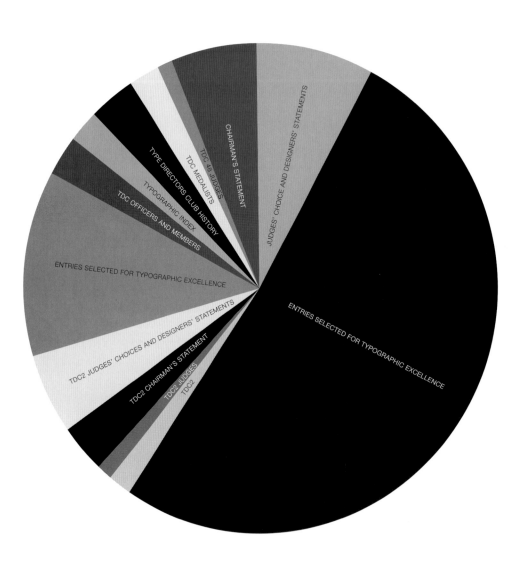

CHAIRMAN'S STATEMENT

JUDGES' CHOICE AND DESIGNERS' STATEMENTS

TDC 48 JUDGES

TDC MEDALISTS

TYPE DIRECTORS CLUB HISTORY

TYPOGRAPHIC INDEX

TDC OFFICERS AND MEMBERS

ENTRIES SELECTED FOR TYPOGRAPHIC EXCELLENCE

ENTRIES SELECTED FOR TYPOGRAPHIC EXCELLENCE

TDC2 JUDGES' CHOICES AND DESIGNERS' STATEMENTS

TDC2 CHAIRMAN'S STATEMENT

TDC2 JUDGES

TDC2

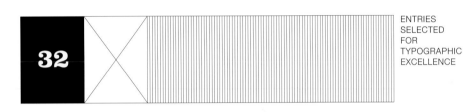

CHAIRMAN
A KLAUS SCHMIDT
  JUDGES
1 PETER BAIN
2 MIRKO ILIĆ
3 SARAH NELSON
4 MARION ENGLISH POWERS
5 GEORGE TSCHERNY
6 KURT WEIDEMANN
7 ALLISON WILLIAMS

JUDGES AND CHAIRMAN(8)

4 892772 383124 2

AAAAAAAAAAAAAAAAAAAAAAAAA

BAIN,PETER[1]CCCCCCCCCCCCCC

DDDDDDDDDDDDDDDDDDDDDDD

EEEEEEEEEEEEFFFFFFFFFFFFFF

GGGGGGGGGGGHHHHHHHHHHH

ILIĆ,MIRKO[2]IIIIIIIIIIIIIIIIIIII

JJJJJJJJJJJJJJJKKKKKKKKKK

LLLLLLLLLLLLLLLLLLLLLLLLL

MMMMMMMMMMMMMMMMMMM

NELSON,SARAH[3]NNNNNNNNN

OOOOOOOOOOOOOOOOOOOOO

POWERS,MARIONENGLISH[4]PPP

QQQQQQQQQQQRRRRRRRRRR

RRRRRRSCHMIDT,KLAUS[a]SSS

SSSSSTSCHERNY,GEORGE[5]TTTT

TTTTTTTTTTTTUUUUUUUUUU

VVVVWEIDEMANN,KURT[6]WW

WILLIAMS,ALLISON[7]XXYYZZZ

OOOOOIIIIII2222223333334444

555556666677777888889 9999

It has been said that typography is the architecture of the printed word because it makes thoughts visible and understandable. As there are manifold ways of laying out a building, there are — nowadays more than ever — varied ways of formulating the typo/graphics of a book, a brochure, a poster, or any media in which print is used.

Over the past decades our Type Directors Club (TDC) shows have convincingly mirrored the ever-changing trends in typography, presenting a panorama of design in print and, more lately, also in electronic media.

As chairman of TDC48, I endeavored to select a jury of professionals with varying viewpoints and experiences in the field of typographic design, a group that would apply their undoubtedly very subjective high standards to selecting not merely newness but excellence in typography. TDC 48, I firmly believe, reflects those varied points of view.

It was my distinct pleasure to work with that conscientious jury of seven (and with TDC Executive Director Carol Wahler whose energy and devotion always contribute greatly toward the success of these competitions). The jury included Peter Bain, like myself one of the last agency type directors; Mirko Ilić, whose specific expertise in letterforms for electronic design contributed immensely; Marion English Powers and Sarah Nelson, both fine typo/graphic designers from Middle America who have been honored with many awards; George Tscherny, a member of the Art Directors Club Hall-of-Fame; Kurt Weidemann, my friend of almost 50 years, who teaches and designs in Germany and who, as I did, acquired a truly tactile feel for type by assembling little leaden characters in a composing stick a long time ago. And last, but not least, that little spitfire of a fine typographic expert, Allison Williams, who is also responsible for this book.

My thanks go to each and every one of them!

Klaus Schmidt is proud of two "Last-of-the-Mohicans" claims — he set metal type by hand and he worked as a real type director. He apprenticed in Germany as a compositor and letterpress printer after World War II, and after immigrating in 1951, he worked in type shops in Detroit and New York City. After graduation from Wayne University, Schmidt became type director at several ad agencies, among them Doyle Dane Bernbach and Young & Rubicam, earning many American and European awards for his typographic work.

Schmidt, who is listed in *Who's Who in America,* joined the Type Directors Club (TDC) more than four decades ago and has been chairman, juror,

and co-coordinator of TDC competitions on numerous occasions. In 1961, he became co-founder, with Aaron Burns, and later chairman of the International Center for the Typographic Arts and helped organize the VISION congresses from 1965 to 1977. He is a past president of the TDC and the Advertising Production Club and vice president of the Art Directors Club of New York. His book, *Signs of the Times,* was published in 1996.

In 1991 Schmidt retired from Young & Rubicam as senior vice president and manager of print and television production and has worked as a consultant since then.

Peter Bain is the principal of Incipit, a practice built on letterforms. Incipit's work encompasses typeface design, logotypes, custom lettering, and typographic design. Clients include Wyeth-Ayerst and The New York Public Library, as well as brand consultants, publishers, and advertising agencies.

Bain's typographic research led him to co-curate the exhibition "Blackletter: Type and National Identity," at the Cooper Union School of Art in New York in 1998. Following that, the exhibit traveled to design conferences in France and Germany. Bain also co-edited the companion monograph published by Princeton Architectural Press. His work on the Blackletter catalog was featured in

Communication Arts and *Baseline* (U.K.) magazines and received awards from the American Institute of Graphic Arts (AIGA) and the Type Directors Club (TDC).

Currently an adjunct instructor of typography at Pratt Institute in Brooklyn, New York, Bain is a member of American Institute of Graphic Arts, the American Printing History Association, and the Association Typographique Internationale (ATypI). He has served on the board of directors for the Society of Scribes and the TDC. Prior to founding Incipit, Bain was type director at Saatchi & Saatchi Advertising in New York for more than a decade.

Mirko Ilić studied illustration and graphic design at the School of Applied Arts in Zagreb. In Europe he illustrated and art directed posters, record covers, and comics. After arriving in the United States in 1986, Ilić was commissioned as an illustrator for many major magazines and newspapers. In 1991 he became art director in charge of the international edition of *Time* magazine, and in 1992 he became art director of *The New York Times* op-ed pages. In 1993 he established and became a partner in Oko & Mano, Inc. In 1995 he established Mirko Ilić Corp., a graphic design, 3-D computer graphics, and motion picture title studio.

Ilić has received medals from the Art Directors Club, *I.D. Magazine*, The Society of Illustrators, the Society of Newspaper Design, the Society of Publication Designers, the Type Directors Club, among others. He was vice president of the New York Chapter of the American Institute of Graphic Arts 1994-1995. Ilić has taught at The Cooper Union with Milton Glaser and teaches masters degree classes in illustration at the School of Visual Arts.

In 2001 Ilić co-authored *Genius Moves: 100 Icons of Graphic Design* with Steven Heller.

Sarah Nelson began her career as a graphic designer by winning the "Keep North Dakota Clean Poster Contest" in 5th grade. Eventually this (along with a lot of other stuff) led her to Werner Design Werks in Minneapolis, where she has been a designer since 1995.

The work of Werner Design ranges from book design, posters, and promotional materials to package design and identity development. The firm's clients include Blu Dot Furniture, Chronicle Books, fX Network, Levi's, Minnesota

Public Radio, Mohawk Paper, MTV Latino, Rizzoli Books, and Target Corp.

Werner Design's work is part of the permanent collection of Toronto's Musee des Arts Decoratifs. The firm has been recognized with awards from American Center for Design, American Institute of Graphic Arts, The Art Directors Club, *Communication Arts, I.D. Magazine, Print Magazine's Regional Design Annual,* and The Type Directors Club. In 1999 Nelson was featured in *Print's* Young Artist Review, Best Artist Under 30.

Marion English Powers is design director of SlaughterHanson. Based in Birmingham, Alabama, SlaughterHanson is primarily a design firm serving national and international clients. A major emphasis of the firm's work is nonprofit organizations as well as corporations whose products or services enhance the human condition. A great deal of Powers' time is spent leading design efforts for cause-related programs. Powers has been at the forefront of a major effort to restore America's oldest baseball park as well as "el nidal" (a garden design project) in one of the poorest sections of Piedras Negras, Mexico.

Powers received her BFA from Auburn University and has work in the permanent collection of the Library of Congress and Museum für Kunst und Gewerbe, Hamburg. Powers is a member of the American Institute of Graphic Arts and the British Design and Art Directors Club. Her work has been published in *The Art Directors Annual, Communication Arts, D&AD, Graphis, Luzer's Archive, One Show,* and *Type Directors Club Annual.*

George Tscherney began his professional career as a designer with Donald Deskey & Associates in 1950. He joined George Nelson & Associates as graphic designer in 1953 and became an associate and head of the graphics department before leaving there in 1955 to open an independent design office.

An extensive selection of Tscherny's work is deposited in the print archive and the electronic database of the Cooper Union School of Art. Over 100 posters and other examples of his work are included in the archives of the Bibliotheque Nationale of France. His posters are represented in the permanent collections of The Museum of Modern Art, New York; The Cooper Hewitt Museum of New York; The Library of Congress,

Washington, D.C.; and the Kunstgewerbemuseum, Zurich.

Tscherney served two terms as president of the American Institute of Graphic Arts and is a member of Alliance Graphique Internationale. In 1988 the American Institute of Graphic Arts awarded George their annual medal "in recognition of distinguished achievements and contributions to the graphic arts."

In 1992 the Visual Arts Museum at the School of Visual Arts invited Tscherney to mount a one-man retrospect of his work in "The Masters Series: honoring the great visual communicators of our time." In 1997 George Tscherney was inducted into the Art Directors Club Hall of Fame.

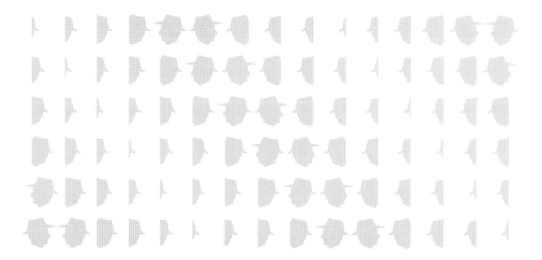

Returning from a Russian POW camp in 1950, Kurt Weidemann served his apprenticeship in a typeshop in the German city of Lübeck and subsequently studied graphic design with Ernst Schneidler at the Academy of Fine Arts, Stuttgart. He returned to that school as a professor after having worked as editor of the German printing magazine, Der Druckspiegel. Weidemann taught design and information techniques for 20 years, after which he worked as an independent book, corporate, and type designer and consultant, forming very close friendships with Georg Trump, Hermann Zapf, Jan Tschichold, Adrian Frutiger, and others.

Kurt Weidemann joined the Type Directors Club in 1966 and served as president of Icograda and of the International Center for Typographic Arts, which was founded by Aaron Burns and Klaus Schmidt in the early 1960s. He has executed corporate design programs for the German Federal Post Office, Daimler-Benz, and numerous other well-known German firms. His typeface designs are ITC Weidemann (a.k.a. Biblica) and Corporate. Since 1990 he has taught at the Design Academy in Karlsruhe, Germany.

Allison Muench Williams and her partner, J. Phillips Williams, founded the New York City-based Design: MW in 1993. The company specializes in establishing the images of such clients as West Elm, Takashimaya New York, and Gmund through collateral, packaging, and interactive work.

Design: MW has received numerous awards internationally for their design work. Highlights include a Gold Clio, Best of Category: Design and Best of Category: Packaging from *I.D. Magazine*, Red Dot:

Best of the Best, Deutscher Preis für Kommunicationsdesign: "Höchste Designqualität," a Silver medal from the Society of Publication Designers, Distinctive Merit Awards from the Art Directors Club, and Critics Choice awards from *Critique* and The Type Directors Club.

A graduate of Rhode Island School of Design, Williams is a visiting critic at Yale University and has lectured and judged competitions throughout the United States.

TDC48
ABBREVIATIONS
2D
2D ANIMATOR
3D
3D ANIMATOR
AM
ANIMATOR
AD
ART DIRECTOR
AG
AGENCY
CA
CATEGORY
CB
CONTRIBUTORS
CD
CREATIVE DIRECTOR
CL
CLIENT
DE
DESIGNER
DM
DIMENSIONS
DS
DESIGN STUDIO
ED
EDITOR
EP
EXECUTIVE PRODUCER
FD
FILM DIRECTOR
FL
FLAME ARTIST
IA
INFERNO ARTIST
IL
ILLUSTRATOR
JD
JUDGE
LT
LETTERING
MS
MUSIC
IN
INSTRUCTOR
PB
PUBLISHER
PD
PRODUCER
PG
PROGRAMMER
PH
PHOTOGRAPHER
PT
PRINTER
TY
PRINCIPAL TYPEFACE
SC
SCHOOL

TDC2
ABBREVIATIONS
CL
CLIENT
DB
DISTRIBUTOR
FA
MEMBERS OF TYPEFACE FAMILY
FD
FOUNDRY
TD
TYPEFACE DESIGNER
TF
TYPEFACE NAME
YR
YEAR OF DESIGN OR RELEASE

JUDGES' CHOICES(7)

JD
PETER BAIN

The modestly sized typographic book is a successful and enduring form, even if graphic designers often overlook what they have in their hands. This book, *Frontier Metropolis: Picturing Early Detroit, 1701-1838,* is in no way modest, yet it more than fulfills the same stringent requirements. The text is not merely legible, but it welcomes the reader. Here one encounters the richness of Fairfield, an appropriately native North American typeface, surrounded by carefully articulated white space. The display headings, years, and marginal notes make pleasing use of the small caps and old style figures, adding variety and gently encouraging any browser to read just a bit further. Taken as a whole, the typographic design is an elegant and efficient navigational aid that presents the historical record on a suitably grand scale. Few table-top books are both for looking and for reading; this is one of them.

DS
STATEMENT

This prephotographic history of Detroit, which was published as part of the city's tricentennial, is told primarily through maps, but also includes documents, portraits, and other artifacts. The maps essentially drove the design/production decisions. Mohawk Superfine was selected to represent the warm, tactile qualities of the original maps. The 18 x 31-inch-page size allowed for large, highly detailed reproductions but also meant the book was a physically challenging volume. To aid readers, dates of each work and figure numbers were placed in the margin for easily reference.

The client, designer, and printer all understood the importance of the project and brought their best to the tale. Ultimately, the project was one of the largest and most satisfying that any of the team had ever worked on. The book was hailed in the press as "the magnum opus of Detroit's tricentennial year."

019

CA
BOOK

DS
WAYNE STATE UNIVERSITY
PRESS

DE
MIKE SAVITSKI
ANN ARBOR MI

AD
MIKE SAVITSKI

PM
ALICE NIGOGHOSIAN

TY
FAIRFIELD

DM
18 X 13 IN
45.7 X 33 CM

The calendar of the year 2002 in format 60 x 81 cm revives poigniant moments through photographs. The photographic works are distinguished by combining provocation with a high level of aestheticism. Photographs become mirrors of retrospection. They help us retrieve personal experiences and oddities out of the dark of our memory. On our journey past the threshold we see ourselves reminded of funny and sad, bizarre and stuffy, comfortable and uncomfortable moments of our lives. They are like emotional snapshots of sports, travel, dining, conversation, competition, or just relaxing — all of them passion-filled moments. The aim of the design is achieved when the beholder is reminded of personal circumstances and experiences.

DS
STATEMENT

Despite its huge size, the calendar Moments of Passion is quite unpretentious. The photography is of mundane things, as if an object of importance is just out of frame. These are the accidental images one gets back and usually throws away. All the typographic elements are on separate pieces of paper, glued to the calendar: an airline luggage tag, the back of a postcard, a supermarket receipt. At first glance, you don't even notice the dates of the calendar, because the type is perfectly adjusted to fit the item.

Altogether they are ephemera — the kinds of things you toss away as you are traveling. You would expect to find these things in the trash or on the floor of the spaces in the photography. To me, the title Moments of Passion is very ironic. It seems like in all of these images, we have just barely missed the passion.

CA
CALENDAR

DS
WWW.VIER-FUER-TEXAS.DE

CL
FACHHOCHSCHULE
WIESBADEN

DE
KLAUS ECKERT
MARCUS MICHAELIS
SEBASTIAN SELL
WIESBADEN GERMANY

PH
KLAUS ECKERT
MARCUS MICHAELIS
SEBASTIAN SELL

DM
23.6 X 31.7 IN
60 X 80.5 CM

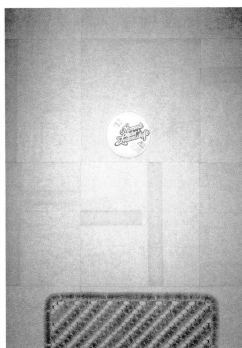

What I particularly liked about the AIGA Design Conference Guide was the dichotomy between the undesigned messages and the beautifully designed book. I love the irony of ugly, pedestrian, handmade signs being used to promote the message of a national design conference. How necessary is graphic design? Isn't just about anyone capable of making some kind of sign to get their message across?

This is a case of the designer literally making use of visual surroundings. Combine that with beautifully simple type and easy-to-access information and you've got a really well-designed conference guide that's not only useful, it's entertaining.

DS
STATEMENT

Maybe we're a bit cynical, but when we heard the theme for the AIGA National Conference was "Voice: Can Design Change the World?" we immediately answered, "No." But as we looked closer, we realized this question was inherently rhetorical. What does "changing the world" really mean? Is it changing the mind of every person on the planet or just one? What is "design" anyway? Visual communication made by a professional graphic designer or a mark made by any person wishing to express an idea?

What does it mean to use one's voice? Are designers using their own or merely embellishing their clients'? To us, voice is first and foremost an individual activity. It can be used to say many kinds of things, but it is essentially an expression in the first person. While most graphic designers — ourselves included — have quieted their own voices in deference to their clients', there are still many examples of individuals making their ideas heard through design. These expressions range from the personal and cryptic to the social and zealous. They are evident in the darkest corners of cities, the playgrounds of the suburbs, and the open spaces of rural areas.

Given the difficulties of affecting people across the globe, we chose to focus on passionate pleas of a smaller scale — from finding a home for a dog to rent control to homelessness. We found just a small sampling in our neighborhood. You will undoubtedly find more by looking around your own city. Ironically, the most powerful work often comes not from marketing expertise or technical virtuosity but from desperation, passion, and honesty. Our hope is that we can all take a cue from these voices and find our own.

CA
BROCHURE

DS
CAHAN & ASSOCIATES

CL
AMERICAN INSTITUTE
OF GRAPHIC ARTS

DE
MICHAEL BRALEY
BOB DINETZ
KEVIN ROBERSON
SHARRIE BROOKS
GARY WILLIAMS
SAN FRANCISCO CA

AD
BILL CAHAN
MICHAEL BRALEY
BOB DINETZ
KEVIN ROBERSON

CD
BILL CAHAN

PH
BOB DINETZ
KEVIN ROBERSON
SHARRIE BROOKS

TY
UNIVERS 55
FRANKLIN GOTHIC

DM
6.75 X 9 IN
17.1 X 22.9 CM

You probably shouldn't say that you selected a favorite piece in a type show because it had soul, but that is exactly why I chose the Sagmeister *Made You Look* book. A work created by Sagmeister Inc., this book is an archive and history of their design work, complete with a "history of the earth" timeline that includes the appearance of graphic design in the earth's history. *Made You Look* starts innocently enough with a red plexi slipcase that reveals a tongue-wagging Rin Tin Tin-type shephard that when slipped from the case turns into a snarling mongrel. Throughout the book the reader finds the smallest bits of wonderful thoughts, diary blurbs, and client quotes handled in varing typographic applications. Hand type, small boxes, type on the edge of the paper, and a dog illustration that runs flip book style along the corner of the page combine to create a humorous adventure to both read and view. Waffling between no restraint and total restraint, the work visually says so much about the client (designer Stefan Sagmeister). A good idea mixed with good type and a very good Norman Rockwell quote. Isn't that what every piece should be?

DS
STATEMENT

Made You Look contains practically all the work we ever designed, including the bad stuff. Removing the book from the red-tinted transparent slip case causes the mood of the dog to worsen considerably. Bending it over results in the title "Made You Look" (or, in the other direction, a picture of dog food) showing up on the fore edge. Peter Hall wrote a very detailed text (for a design book), and I included handwritten excerpts from my diary and many comments from our dear clients.

CA
BOOK

DS
SAGMEISTER INC.

CL
BOOTH-CLIBBORN EDITIONS

DE
STEFAN SAGMEISTER
HJALTI KARLSSON
NEW YORK NY

AD
STEFAN SAGMEISTER

CD
STEFAN SAGMEISTER

CW
PETER HALL

PH
KEVIN KNIGHT

TY
SPARTAN
NEWS GOTHIC
HANDLETTERING

DM
9.5 X 7 IN
24.1 X 17.8 CM

Selecting material for a type exhibition presents conflicts in judgment. The reason is that it is not a design show and not a photography show and not an illustration show. Yet, to some degree, one or all of these aspects are likely to be present in the pieces being viewed. As a consequence some border-line cases may well have found their way into the show.

There can be no confusion about the inclusion of the Paul Newman poster. It is clearly a typographic solution. While there is the presence of a photographic portrait, it is subordinated to the bold handling of the type.

Justification for singling this piece out for comment is really based on the ingenious treatment of the Newman name. It is a perfect example of *the found object in art,* requiring scavenger eyes to find it.

DS
STATEMENT

Working for a repertory cinema, I have to deal repeatedly with an uncomfortable situation: I have to write on a poster what is shown and I have to show on it what is written. That was the case with this poster, since the client insisted on showing a photograph of Paul Newman.

As stars are not unknown people, the image and the name somehow become synonyms. To avoid banality, I took banality as the topic of my visualization. The face is shown by the name and the name is formed by the face. Of course, I was very lucky Paul's surname is Newman.

CA
POSTER

DS
SCHRAIVOGEL

CL
FILM PODIUM ZURICH

PT
ALBIN ULDRY
HINTERKAPPELEN
SWITZERLAND

DE
RALPH SCHRAIVOGEL
ZURICH SWITZERLAND

AD
RALPH SCHRAIVOGEL

CD
RALPH SCHRAIVOGEL

LT
RALPH SCHRAIVOGEL

TY
FRANKLIN GOTHIC

DM
35.6 X 50.4 IN
90.5 X 128 CM

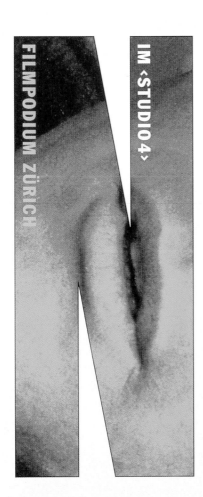
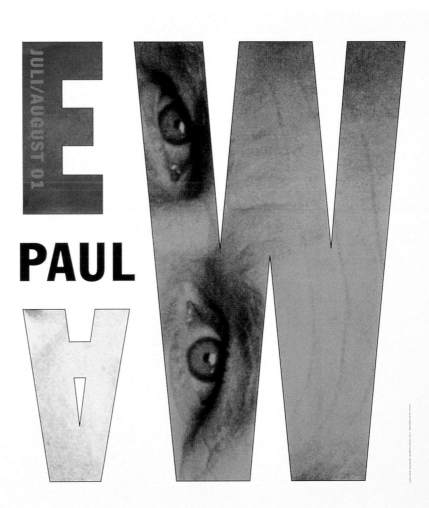

A young Dutch enterprise, operating in the realm of internationally oriented financial services, engaged three youthful Amsterdam designers for its annual business report. The design team does not merely believe in the beauty and expressiveness of good typography but also delivers convincing proof of those attributes. The report is printed on a rather unpretentious 80 gram stock with a modest flexible cover. The layout arrangements are logical and full of delightful variations. Color is used as a stimulating, invigorating element — not indiscriminately interspersed but employed to support the information. Type sizes, setting widths, as well as display arrangements vary and abide by the accepted rules of readability. The photographic illustrations are rendered in skillfully unregistered process colors. The design presents a sympathetic business company that permits ideas to dominate over extravagance.

DS
STATEMENT

Delta Lloyd Nuts Ohra is a leading financial services provider in Northwest Europe, offering financial products and services focused on asset accumulation, income protection, and risk management. For their 2000 annual report the design firm UNA developed a clear (typo)-graphic structure that promotes accessibility to the various categories of texts and figures. The holding consists of eight divisions, all of which present their results. This requires a clearly visible segmentation. The same goes for the annual accounts: strong contrast distinguishes between accounts and notes to the accounts.

2000 was the first complete financial year after the merger of Delta Lloyd and Nuts Ohra. The annual report features the importance of entrepreneurial employees and team spirit within the new company. Managers and board members were asked to present their vision on the phenomena of enterprise, and illustrations show these managers and board members with their staffs.

CA
ANNUAL REPORT

DS
UNA (AMSTERDAM)
DESIGNERS

CL
DELTA LLOYD NUTS OHRA

DE
HANS BOCKTING
WILL DE L'ECLUSE
SABINE REINHARDT
AMSTERDAM
THE NETHERLANDS

TY
SWIFT

DM
9.1 X 11.6 IN
23 X 29.5 CM

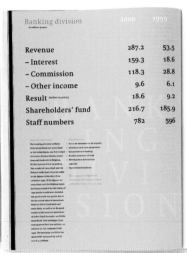

Strategy and development 'Our banking activities have been reorganised. Our new mission: Excel in niches'

Hans Eric Jansen, Chairman of the Executive Board Delta Lloyd Nuts Ohra

Enterprise

Enterprise for me is: take initiatives, solve a problem, see that things happen, don't wait for it, do it. Enterprise means dynamics, flair. Enterprise is fun. When an entrepreneurial wind is blowing through a company, the company is to become good as a matter of course. Customers are being served rapidly and properly, plans are realised, staff is motivated. Americans like to call this a 'happy company'. There is no choice for me: Delta Lloyd Nuts Ohra means enterprise; it is good for everybody. And who does not like to work for a 'happy company'?

JD
ALLISON WILLIAMS

Out of the rich and varied entries in this year's TDC competition, I never thought that I would pick a self-promotional calendar by a design firm as my "judge's choice." The last thing the world needs is more designers' self-promo pieces, and desktop calendars seem particularly uninspiring and useless. But other than the calendar vehicle (which I learned from the statement below is a continuation of a 10-year series) this piece transcends so many of the design cliches used within it: featherweight stock printed on the reverse side, perforations, blind embossing, 4 point type, type used as textural wallpaper, etc., etc., and triple etc. Overwhelmingly understated — a book waiting to be peeked into, explored, caressed, violated, and ultimately desecrated in the service of you. A tasty morsel; the ultimate seduction.

DS
STATEMENT

For more than a decade UNA (Amsterdam) designers and their associates have initiated and produced desk diaries intended as gifts for their respective business clients. For many of the recipients these diaries are valued as collectors' items.

"Marking Time" is the title of the 2002 diary. The concept celebrates the manifold events, occasions, holidays, and anniversaries around the world. Each week commemorates a significant holiday — religious, secular, legendary, historical, political — observed in that week by one of the world's many nations. A relevant story is told — visually and verbally — in a sometimes humorous, sometimes ironic way. Collectively, the fifty-two stories represent a unique and provocative history of people marking time. As the year progresses, your own story of marking time will be told as well.

CA
CALENDAR

DS
UNA (AMSTERDAM)
DESIGNERS

CL
UNA (AMSTERDAM)
DESIGNERS
BINDERIJ HEXSPOOR
MEGHAN FERRILL
VEENMAN DRUKKERS

DE
ANDRÉ CREMER
WILL DE L'ECLUSE
AMSTERDAM
THE NETHERLANDS

CW
MEGHAN FERRILL

TY
BELL CENTENNIAL

DM
7.7 X 9.5 IN
19.5 X 24 CM

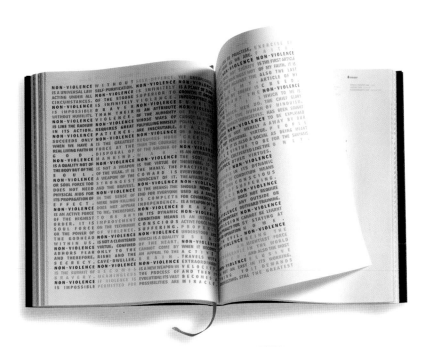

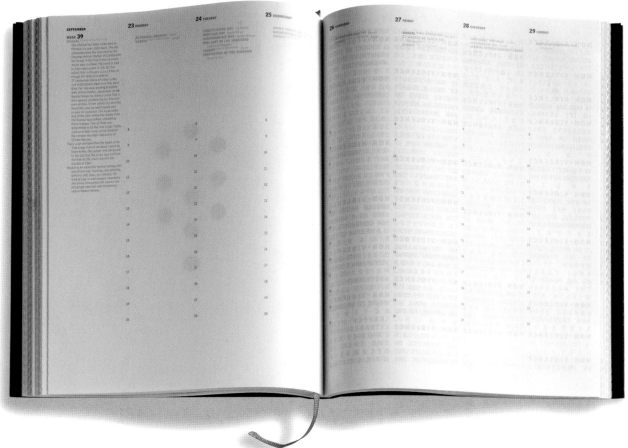

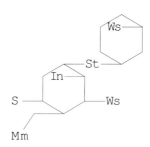

TDC48

(Pb) (148)   Publication

(Mm) (7)   Multimedia

(Bk) (Book)
(Ci) (Corporate Identity)
(Ed) (Editorial)
(P)   (Poster)
(Pb) (Publication)
(Pk) (Packaging)
(St) (Student)

(In) (Interactive)
(Ws) (Web Site)
(S)   (Signage System)
(St) (Student)
(Mm) (Multimedia)

$$TDC_{48}Winners = P_{26}Pb_{92}S_3Pk_6M_7Ci_{19}St_{12}$$

CA
SIGNAGE

DS
CONCRETE DESIGN
COMMUNICATIONS INC.

CL
ADVERTISING AND
DESIGN CLUB OF CANADA

DE
JOHN PYLYPCZAK
THERESA KWAN
TORONTO CANADA

AD
JOHN PYLYPCZAK
DITI KATONA

CW
JOHN PYLYPCZAK
STEPHEN BLAIR

TY
INTERSTATE

DM
VARIOUS

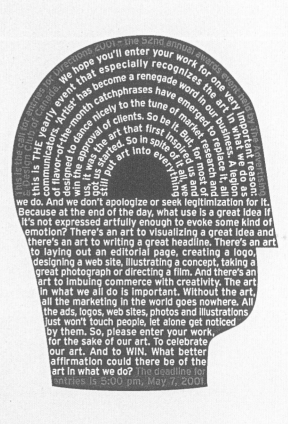

A+D

The Board of Directors of The Advertising and Design Club of Canada would like to thank you for participating in Directions 2001 – our 52nd annual awards show. You entered the show because you believe there is "art" in what we all do as communicators. You believe that merely communicating an idea is not sufficient if those ideas are not communicated artfully enough to evoke strong emotions. Because without the art, all the marketing in the world goes nowhere. All the ads, logos, web sites, photos and illustrations just won't touch people, let alone get noticed by them. You also entered because you respect our roster of international judges – your peers on the global stage. Their work represents the standard to which we all aspire. They have demonstrated that there truly is an art to imbuing commerce with creativity. We aspire to that same standard and we value what they have to say. Now they have spoken. This show contains what our judges consider to be the best work in the country – our extended creative community. It is the work that goes beyond simply satisfying creative briefs and market research findings. It expresses something much more – something that has the ability to move and touch people. So please attend our show to see the work that has won and to celebrate the art in what we do. Directions 2001 will take place Friday, November 16 at 6:30 pm at the Design Exchange. Tickets are on sale now.

DIRECTIONS 2001 To encourage and promote the highest professional standards, The Advertising & Design Club of Canada's annual show and awards presentation salutes the best of this year's creative work, selected by an internationally recognized jury of experienced judges. Winning work is displayed at the show and also published in the awards annual as a permanent record. Gold and silver medal selections will become part of the collection of the Royal Ontario Museum. The deadline for entries is 5:00 p.m., May 7, 2001

A+D

Advertising Print

Advertising Broadcast

Advertising Multiple Media

Graphic Design

Advertising Broadcast Crafts for Television and Cinema Commercials

Editorial Design

CA
ANNUAL REPORT

CL
SILICON VALLEY BANK

DS
CAHAN & ASSOCIATES

DE
MICHAEL BRALEY
SAN FRANCISCO CA

AD
BILL CAHAN
MICHAEL BRALEY

CD
BILL CAHAN

PH
JOCK MCDONALD
GRAHAM MACINDOE

TY
NEUE HELVETICA

DM
6.5 X 11 IN
16.5 X 27.9 CM

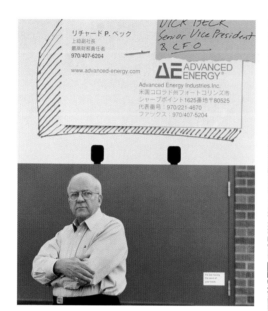

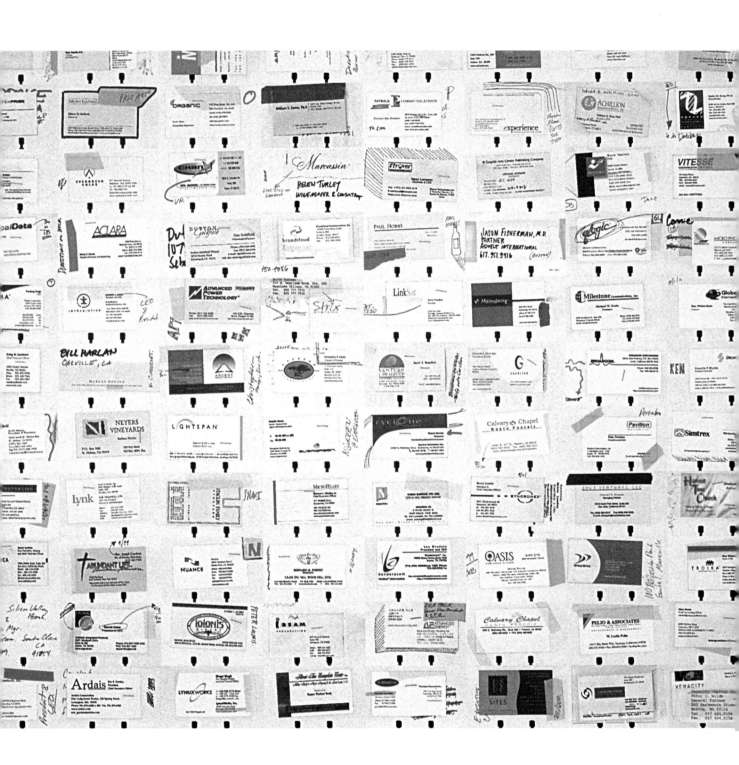

CA
POSTER

DS
KARLSSONWILKER INC.

DE
HJALTI KARLSSON
JAN WILKER
NEW YORK NY

AD
HJALTI KARLSSON
JAN WILKER

CD
HJALTI KARLSSON
JAN WILKER

CW
HJALTI KARLSSON
JAN WILKER

TY
DIN

DM
23 X 32 IN
58.4 X 81.3 CM

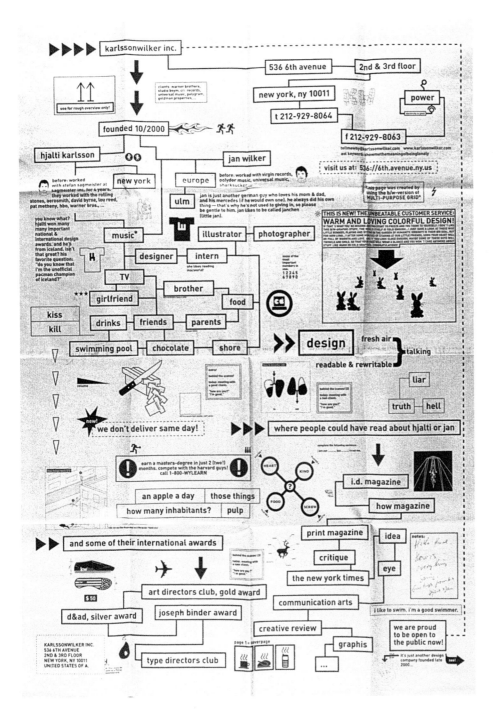

CA
POSTER

DS
SHINMURA DESIGN OFFICE

CL
SHINMURA FISHERIES

DE
NORITO SHINMURA
TOKYO JAPAN

AD
NORITO SHINMURA

LT
NORITO SHINMURA

PH
KIYOFUSA NOZU

TY
HANDMADE

DM
40.6 X 28.75 IN
103 X 7.3 CM

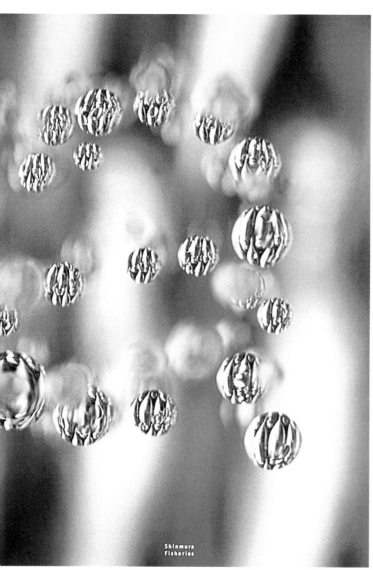

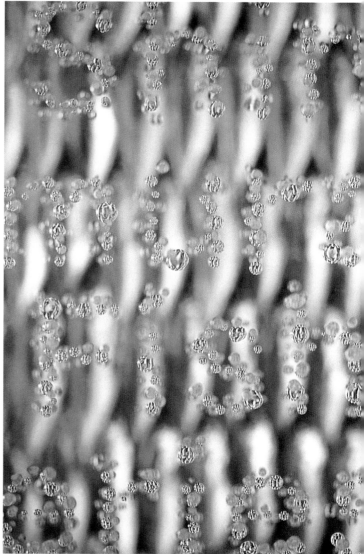

Shinmura
Fisheries

CA
ANNUAL REPORT

CL
ROYAL SOCIETY OF ARTS

DS
ATELIER WORKS

DE
IAN CHILVERS
ALEXANDRA COE
LONDON ENGLAND

AD
IAN CHILVERS

TD / IL
DEREK BIRDSALL
MIKE DEMPSEY
ALAN FLETCHER
MALCOLM GARRETT
ALAN KITCHING
JOHN MCCONNELL
PIERRE MENDELL

TY
GILL SANS

DM
11 X 9 IN
28 X 23 CM

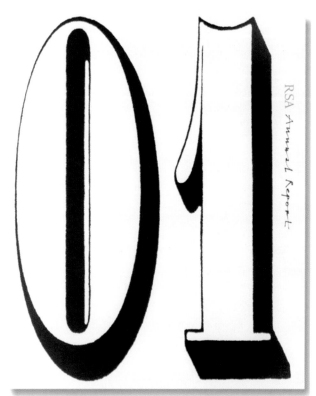

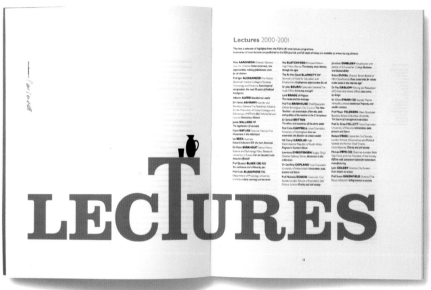

DS
PENTAGRAM

CL
TAYLOR WILSON PUBLISHING

DE
D. J. STOUT
JULIE SAVASKY
AUSTIN TX

AD
D. J. STOUT

TY
TYPEKA BOLD
CASLON 540

DM
4.75 X 7 IN
12.1 X 17.8 CM

CA
POSTER

CL
MORISAWA CO., LTD.

DS
STUDIO FUKU-DE

DE
HIDEYUKI FUKUDA
TOKYO JAPAN

AD
HIDEYUKI FUKUDA

CD
HIDEYUKI FUKUDA

TY
MB101

DM
40.6 X 57.3 IN
103 X 145.6 CM

CA
POSTER

DS
STUDIO FUKU-DE

CL
JAPAN GRAPHIC DESIGNERS
ASSOCIATION INC

DE
HIDEYUKI FUKUDA
TOKYO JAPAN

AD
HIDEYUKI FUKUDA

CD
HIDEYUKI FUKUDA

TY
HELVETICA
MB101

DM
40.6 X 28.7 IN
103 X 72.8 CM

CA
POSTER

CL
LABOR FÜR SOZIALE UND
ÄSTHETISCHE
ENTWICKLUNGEN

DS
FONS HICKMANN M23

DE
FONS M. HICKMANN
BERLIN GERMANY

AD
FONS M. HICKMANN

CW
THORSTEN NOLTING

TY
HELVETICA

DM
33.1 X 23.6 IN
84 X 60 CM

2. Reihe: **Got it?**

Freie Reden mit christlichem Unterton

Thorsten Nolting

Montag bis Freitag 18. Februar bis 31. März

15 Uhr Nachdenklich

16 Uhr Bei der Arbeit

17 Uhr Im Getümmel

18 Uhr Natürlich

Foto: Fons M. Hickmann

Labor für soziale und ästhetische Entwicklung

Berger Kirche, Bergerstrasse Ecke Wallstrasse, Düsseldorf

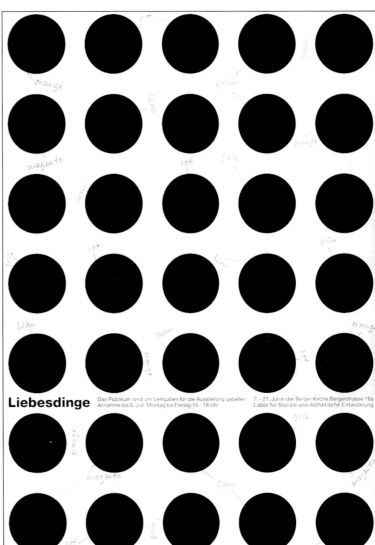

CA
BOOK COVER

DS
COMPAÑÍA

CL
EDITORIAL CRÍTICA

DE
XAVIER BANÚS
ARMANDO FIDALGO
BARCELONA SPAIN

AD
XAVIER BANÚS
ARMANDO FIDALGO

CD
XAVIER BANÚS
ARMANDO FIDALGO

TY
SACKERS GOTHIC
FF SCALA

DM
4.75 X 7.7 IN
12.1 X 19.5 CM

ROMANCERO

6 NADA

7 LIBRO DE BUEN AMOR

8 LEYENDAS

12 DON JUAN TENORIO

crítica

crítica

crítica

crítica

crítica

CARMEN LAFORET

ARCIPRESTE DE HITA

GUSTAVO ADOLFO BÉCQUER

JOSÉ ZORRILLA

CA
ANNUAL REPORT

CL
MAXYGEN

DS
CAHAN & ASSOCIATES

DE
GARY WILLIAMS
SAN FRANCISCO CA

AD
BILL CAHAN
GARY WILLIAMS

CD
BILL CAHAN

PH
ANN GIORDANO
ESTHER HENDERSON
RAY MANLEY
ROBERT MARKOW
JOHN SANN

TY
MINION
TRADE GOTHIC

DM
7 X 10 IN
17.8 X 25.4 CM

Maxygen is working to create new and improved products and
processes for the chemical industry.

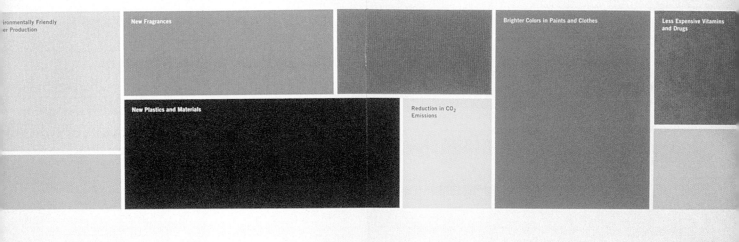

ironmentally Friendly
er Production

New Fragrances

Brighter Colors in Paints and Clothes

Less Expensive Vitamins
and Drugs

New Plastics and Materials

Reduction in CO_2
Emissions

CA
BOOK

DS
LAMBERT UND LAMBERT

CL
DÜSSELDORFER
SCHAUSPIELHAUS

DE
MIRIAM LAMBERT
NINA LAMBERT
DÜSSELDORF GERMANY

TY
TRADE GOTHIC CONDENSED
FF SCALA REGULAR
UNIVERS 57 CONDENSED

DM
4.8 X 7.75 IN
12.2 X 19.7 CM

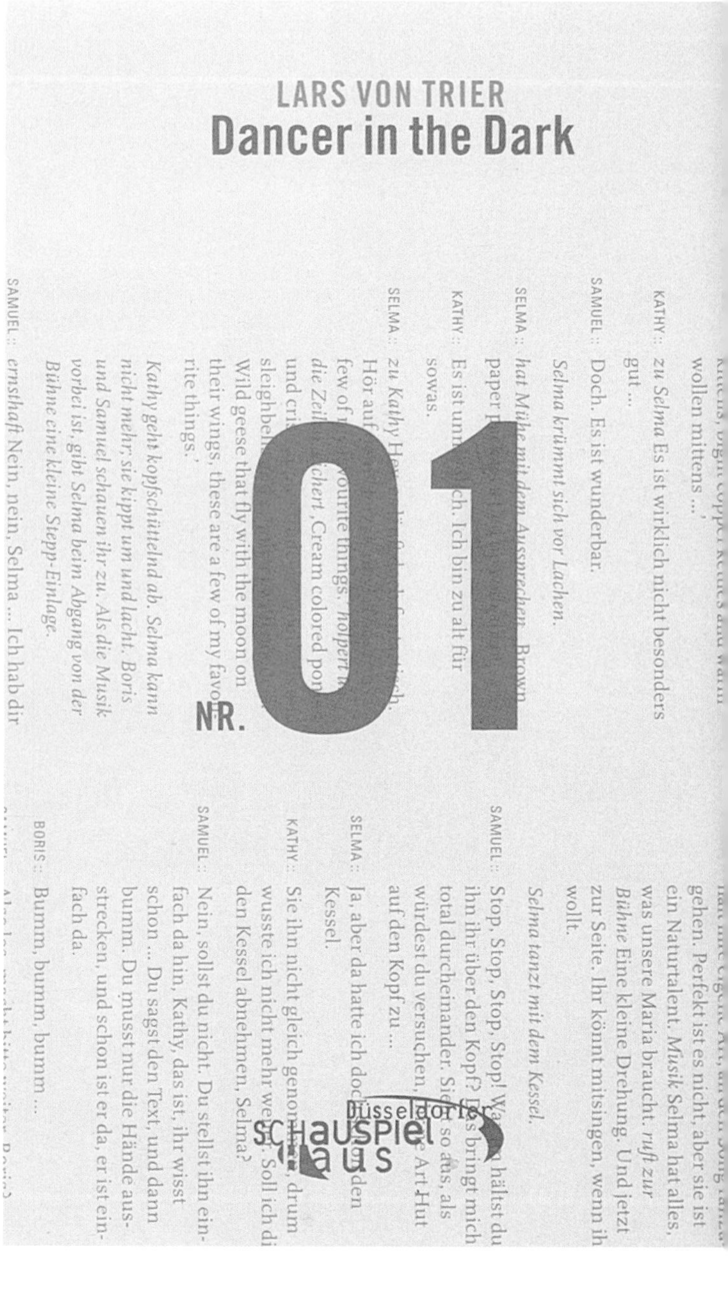

LARS VON TRIER
Dancer in the Dark

NR. **01**

schauspiel haus
Düsseldorfer

JON FOSSE
Da kommt noch wer

SIE:: muter
Jetzt sind wir bald in unserem Haus
ER:: Unser Haus
SIE:: Ein schönes altes Haus
Weit weg von anderen Häusern
und von anderen Leuten
SIE:: Du und ich allein
ER:: Nicht nur allein
sondern allein [...]
blickt in sein Ge[...]
Unser Haus
In diesem Haus wo [...]
du und ich
allein mitenan[...]
ER:: Und niemand [...]
kommen
SIE:: Sie bleiben steh[...]
ER:: Jetzt sind wir bei unserem Haus angekommen
SIE:: Jetzt sind wir bei unserem Haus angekommen
ER:: Das Haus ist ja doch hübsch

NR. 02

Jetzt sind wir bei unserem Haus angekommen
Bei unserem Haus
wo wir allein sein werden
Du und ich allein
bei dem Haus
wo du und ich allein sein werden

Das Haus ist ja doch hübsch
mit dem Regen und der Dunkelheit
im Dunkeln
wie das im Herbst wird
stell dir vor
wie die Wellen schlagen
und stell dir vor
wie das Meer weiß und schwarz ist
wenn die Wellen hoch schlagen
wenn du das Meer tosen hörst
durch die Wände pfeift
wenn der Wind
Und stell dir vor wenn es dunkel wird
nachdrücklicher
Stell dir vor wenn ein Gewitter kommt

und jetzt stehen wir vor diesem Haus und

Düsseldorfer
schauspiel Haus

IGOR BAUERSIMA
Launischer Sommer

Ufer des Flusses.

ABBÉ: Nachdem der Bademeister Anton an diesem
Vormittag also sein Lied zu Ende gesungen
hat, tritt er heraus, verschränkt die Hände auf
dem Rücken und pustet unwillkürlich auf das
Kölbchen des Thermometers. Diese so gut wie
unbestechliche Säule jedoch bewe[...]
kaum, und Anto[...]
Redlichkeit [...]
ablösen wie d[...] [...] bein [...]
Die Beschaffe[...] [...]es Sommers,
mir einigermaßen [...] glücklich. Es ist
mein Atem ist fr[...]
uns, wenn nic[...]
für Gesundhe[...] [...]körperliche Reinlich[...]
zu sorgen? N[...] [...]nn, mag die Witterung [...]
stig sein oder[...]
Aufschub.

So spricht der Meister, schnallt sein Tuch a[...]
tut einen Schritt ins Wasser, das seine lange [...]
behaarten Beine, die Einfassung des Bassins
und das Himmelsgewölbe spiegelt, gewahrt
darin das Bild eines umgekippten Gefäßes, das
jemand zu dicht an den Rand gestellt hatte und
fügt hinzu:

ANTON: Ach, das Schwimmbad ist leer und dieses
Gefäß auch.

NR. 03

ABBÉ: Ich lasse mich auf dem Steinwall nieder und
antworte, gelinde schmählend, doch nicht die
Grenzen des wohlanständigen Gesprächs
überschreitend. Was sind Sie doch für ein sau-
beres Geziefer, der Sie Ihre [...] so unbe-
schwert ablegen wie ein eh[...]er Mann seine
Mütze? Wer war Ihr Lehr[...] Wer hat Ihnen sol-
che Sitten beigebracht?

ANTON: Mir wurden gesundheitsf[...] Ansichten
eingepflanzt, ich habe sie a[...]ommen und
achte ihrer zum großen Nutz[...] meinen
Leib. Scheren Sie sich von da[...] mit Ihren
Buch der Oden und ihrem Frie[...] der abge-
nutzt und stumpf an den Zeit[...] kratzt, ohne
deren Sinn erfassen zu können. Gehen Sie, Sie
Erläuterer von Schändlichkeiten, geschwätzi-
gen Lettern und schwermütigen Zeiten, die
sich in den Kopf gesetzt haben, nach allen
Regeln der Kunst zu hinken. Ich bin hier um
Ihnen auf alle Verleumdungen zu antworten,
mit denen Sie mich seit fünf Jahren überschüt-
ten, aber meine Hand ist nass und es ist zu
spät, die Zigarre aus dem Munde zu nehmen.

möchte nur allzu gern einige Wahrheiten aus-
sprechen, die man sich zur rechten Zeit anhö-
ren muss.

Anton lässt sich langsam ins Wasser gleiten.

Düsseldorfer
schauspiel Haus

CA
CORPORATE IDENTITY

CL
MUNKEDALS AB

DS
HAPPY FORSMAN &
BODENFORS

DE
MARC EASTMOND
GOTHENBURG SWEDEN

AD
ANDREAS KITTEL

CD
ANDERS KORNESTEDT
BJÖRN ENGSTRÖM

TY
AVENIR

DM
VARIOUS

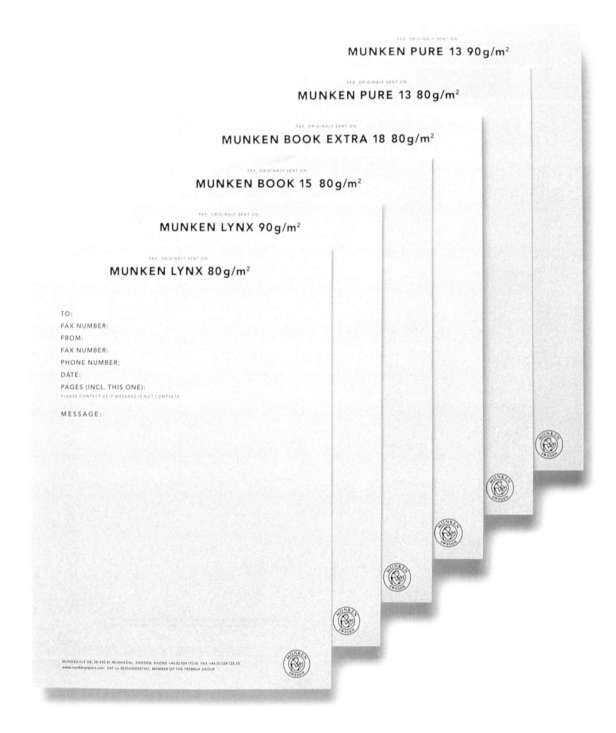

EVA-LENA PETERSSON
Area Sales Manager

MUNKEDALS AB, SE-455 81 MUNKEDAL, SWEDEN
PHONE +46 (0) 524 170 00, FAX +46 (0) 524 134 66
DIRECT PHONE +46 (0) 524 172 78
MOBILE PHONE +46 (0) 705 41 14 81
E-MAIL evalena.petersson@munkedals.se
www.munkenpapers.com

MEMBER OF THE TREBRUK GROUP

MUNKEN PRINT 15 300g/m^2

MUNKEN PURE 11 240g/m^2

MUNKEN PURE 11 300g/m^2

MUNKEN LYNX 300g/m^2

MUNKEN LYNX 240g/m^2

MUNKEN PRINT EXTRA 15 300g/m^2

MUNKEN PURE 13 100g/m^2

MUNKEN LYNX 115g/m^2

MUNKEN LYNX 100g/m^2

CA
BROCHURE

CL
KAAS TAILORED

DS
GRAPHICA COMMUNICATION
SOLUTIONS

DE
CHRISTA FLEMING
SEATTLE WA

AD
CRAIG TERRONES

CD
CRAIG TERRONES

PH
PATRICK BARTA

TY
GILL SANS

DM
6.5 X 8 IN
16.5 X 20.3 CM

CA
CATALOG

DS
HAPPY FORSMAN &
BODENFORS

CL
RÖHSSKA MUSEUM

DE
ANDREAS KITTEL
GOTHENBURG SWEDEN

AD
ANDREAS KITTEL

CD
ANDERS KORNESTEDT

LT
ULF BECKMAN
INGRID SOMMAR

TY
AKZIDENZ GROTESK
ADOBE GARAMOND

DM
9.25 X 7.3 IN
23.6 X 18.5 CM

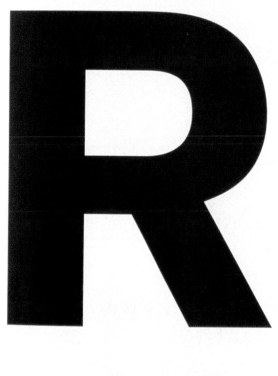

CA
CALENDAR

DS
SIGN*

DE
OLIVIER STÉNUIT
FRANCK SARFATI
JOËL VAN AUDENHAEGE
BRUSSELS BELGIUM

TY
GARAMOND
GARAMOND EXPERT

DM
5.8 X 7.4 IN
14.8 X 18.8 CM

CA
BOOK

CL
WHITE ARCHITECTS

DS
HAPPY FORSMAN &
BODENFORS

DE
ANTON NORDSTIERNA
GAVIN SMART
GOTHENBURG SWEDEN

AD
LISA CAREBORG

CD
ANDERS KORNESTEDT

LT
KATJA GRILLNER
FREDRIK NILSSON

TY
AKZIDENZ GROTESK

DM
8.3 X 6.7 IN
21 X 17 CM

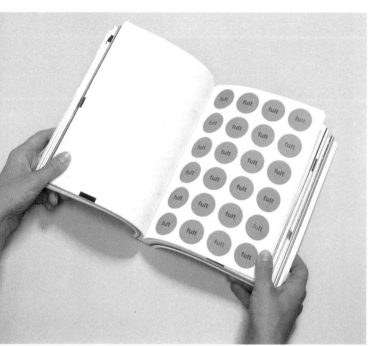

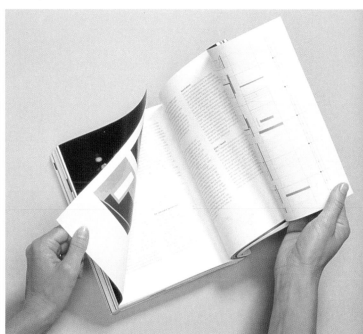

CA
BUSINESS CARDS

DS
SENSUS DESIGN FACTORY

DE
NEDJELJKO SPOLJAR
ZAGREB CROATIA

AD
NEDJELJKO SPOLJAR

CW
KRISTINA SPOLJAR

TY
FF PROFILE

DM
3.2 X 2 IN
8 X 5 CM

CA
CATALOG

CL
OJI PAPER CO., LTD.

DS
KOKOKUMARU INC.

DE
YOSHIMARU TAKAHASHI
OSAKA JAPAN

AD
YOSHIMARU TAKAHASHI

TY
TEGAMI

DM
11.8 X 11.8 IN
30 X 30 CM

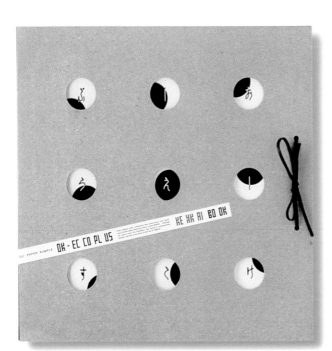

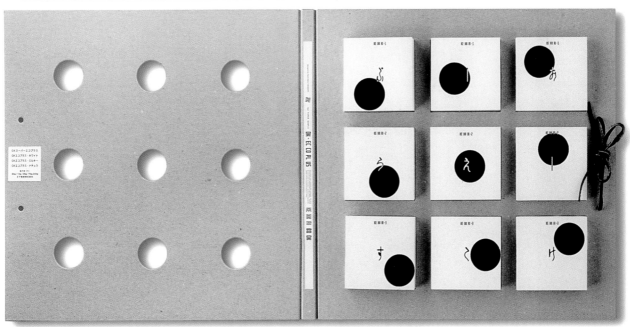

CA
SIGNAGE

CL
EICHER SIEBDRUCK AND
REINHARD EICHER

DE
MARKUS FISCHER
BURKHARD WITTEMEIER
ANDREAS UEBELE
STUTTGART GERMANY

TY
FF DIN

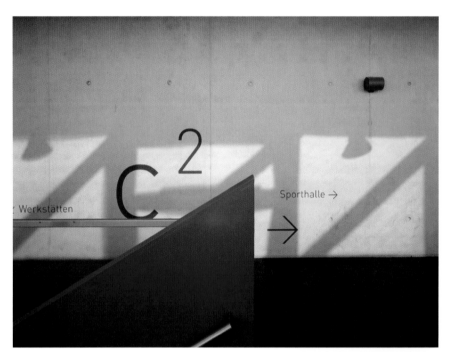

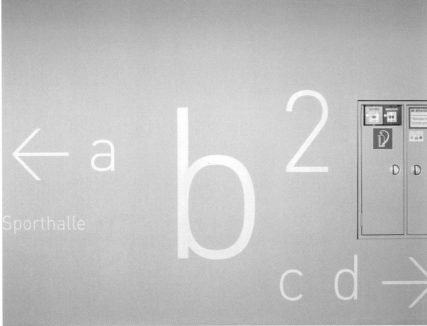

CA
BOOK

DS
LETTERBOX

DE
STEPHEN BANHAM
MELBOURNE AUSTRALIA

TY
SUPER GROTESK
FORTIES
BERBER
MONTAN

DM
5.25 X 5.25 IN
14.5 X 14.5 CM

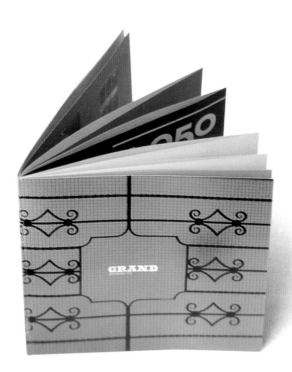

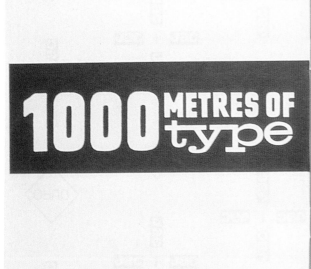

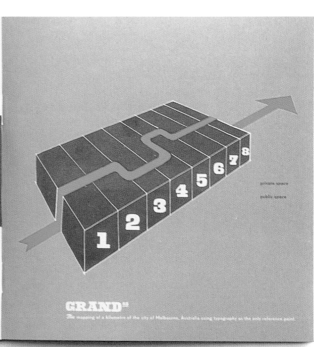

CA
CALENDAR

DS
ZITROMAT

DE
BERIT KAISER
PHILIPP VON ROHDEN
BERLIN GERMANY

TY
FRENCH SCRIPT
ITC CONDUIT

DM
11.7 X 16.5 IN
29.7 X 42 CM

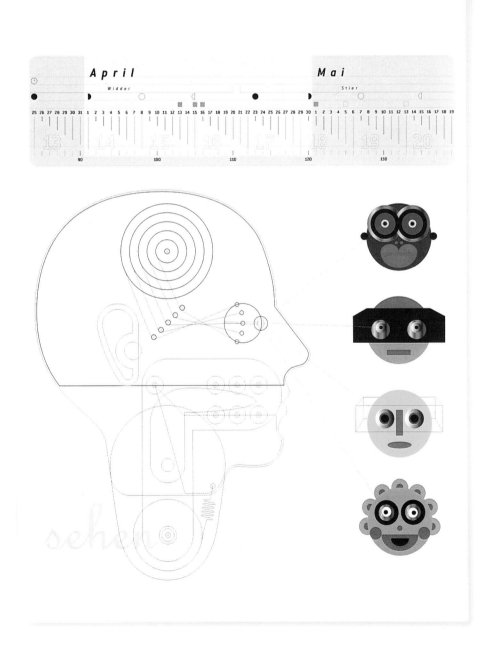

CA
MAGAZINE

DS
MUTABOR DESIGN

AG
PETER GROSCHUPF BRAND
COMMUNICATIONS

CL
PREMIER AUTOMOTIVE
GROUP, LONDON

DE
DANIEL BOGNAR
SIMONE CAMPE
CHRISTIAN DWORAK
MARION FINK
JESSICA HOPPE
STEFANIE TOMAJEK
HAMBURG GERMANY

AD
PAUL NEULINGER

TY
CARPLATE
DTL HAARLEMMER
MONOTYPE GROTESQUE

DM
11.6 X 9.1 IN
29.5 X 23 CM

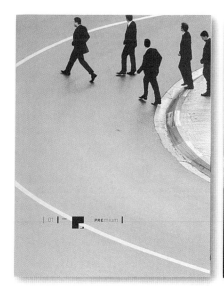

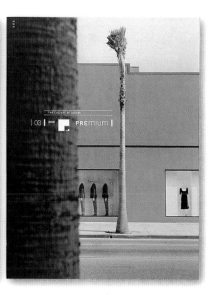

CULT OF
KOI

Its milky scales shimmer as if they were made of Chinese porcelain; from head to tail it is a perfect example of aesthetic symmetry, with a body tapered elegantly like a torpedo; its pectoral fins are reminiscent of open fans. This is not just a fish, it is a living, swimming work of art.

FEATURE

CA
CALENDAR

DS
ARKZIN D.O.O.

CL
IGEPA PLANA PAPERS

DE
DEJAN KRŠIĆ
DEJAN DRAGOSAVAC RUTTA
ZAGREB CROATIA

TY
QUADRAAT
VARIOUS

DM
18.9 X 26.8 IN
48 X 68 CM

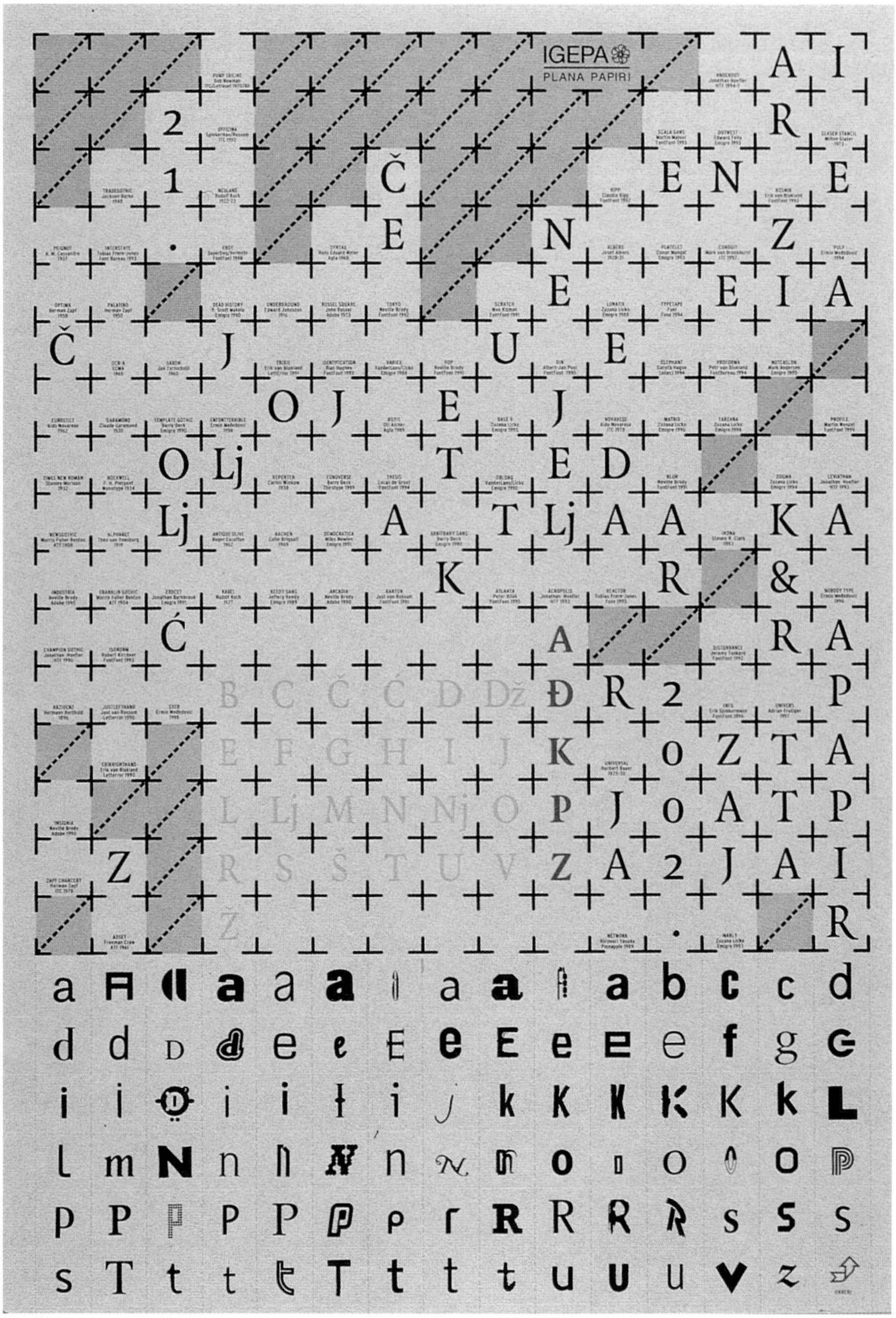

CA
POSTER

DS
FACHHOCHSCHULE
DORTMUND
FONS HICKMANN M23

CL
FACHHOCHSCHULE
DORTMUND

DE
CHRISTOPH BEBERMEIER
THOMAS ARMBORST
BERLIN GERMANY

AD
CHRISTOPH BEBERMEIER
THOMAS ARMBORST

CD
FONS M. HICKMANN
HEIMER SCHMITZ

TY
VAN DOESBERG
AKZIDENZ GROTESK BOLD

DM
47.2 X 33.1 IN
120 X 84 CM

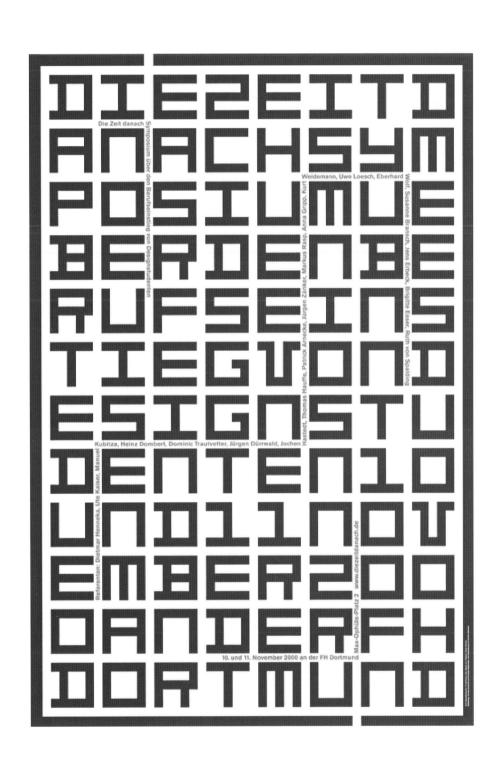

CA
CATALOG

CL
ALT SPEC

DS
TOLLESON DESIGN

DE
STEVE TOLLESON
JOHN BARRETTO
SAN FRANCISCO CA

AD
STEVE TOLLESON

TY
DIN MITTELSCHRIFT
TRADE GOTHIC

DM
9 X 12.25 IN
22.9 X 31.1 CM

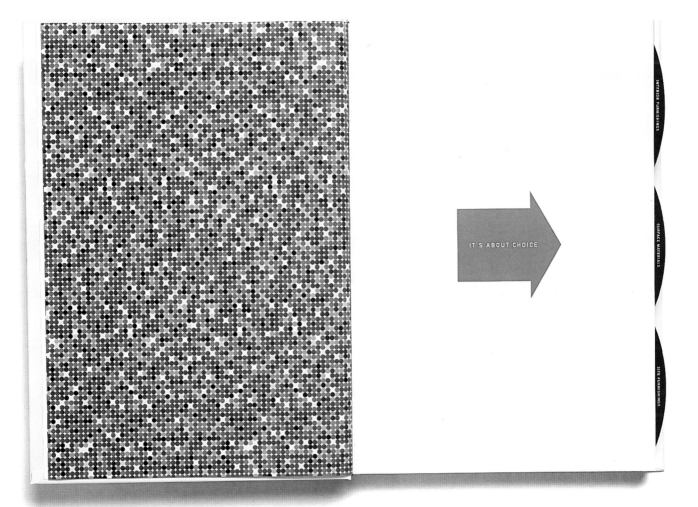

IT'S ABOUT CHOICE

INTERIOR FURNISHINGS

SURFACE MATERIALS

SITE FURNISHINGS

CA
ANNUAL REPORT

CL
HERMAN MILLER, INC.

DS
BBK STUDIO

DE
STEPHEN FRYKHOLM
ZEELAND MI
YANG KIM
GRAND RAPIDS MI

AD
STEPHEN FRYKHOLM

CD
STEPHEN FRYKHOLM

IL
YANG KIM
MICHELE CHARTIER

CW
CLARK MALCOLM

TY
AVENIR

DM
8.5 X 11 IN
21.6 X 27.9 CM

2001 FORM 10-K
HERMAN MILLER, INC., AND SUBSIDIARIES

2001 PROXY STATEMENT AND
NOTICE OF ANNUAL MEETING OF SHAREHOLDERS

2001 REPORT TO SHAREHOLDERS
HERMAN MILLER, INC., AND SUBSIDIARIES

AT HERMAN MILLER,
INNOVATION IS A PROCESS OF DISCOVERY.
IT BEGINS WITH THE MOST UNLIKELY THINGS

⊕HermanMiller

CUSTOMERS WITH NO BUDGET
IMPATIENCE

THE COMPANY MILLWRIGHT
AN AFTER DINNER SPEECH

THE N-GENERATION
TWO MIDDLE-AGED AMERICAN DESIGNERS
MISTAKES

U.S. ARMY ANTHROPOMETRIC STUDIES
HOSPITAL BED
THE U.S. NAVY

CA
BROCHURE

DS
HAEFELINGER + WAGNER
DESIGN

DE
KERSTIN WEIDEMEYER
MUNICH GERMANY

TY
BANK GOTHIC
SWIFT LIGHT

CL
ROHI STOFFE GMBH

CD
KERSTIN WEIDEMEYER

DM
10.2 X 7.5 IN
26 X 19 CM

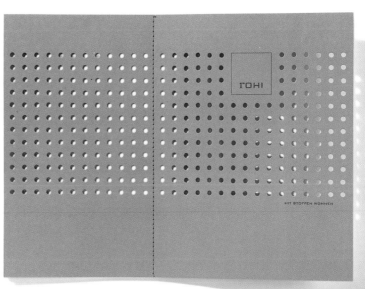

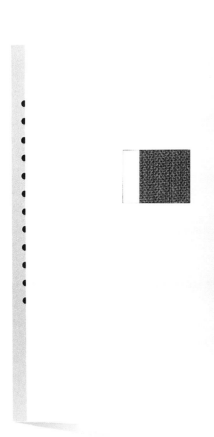

CA
ADVERTISEMENT

AG
RECRUIT CO., LTD.

DS
E. CO., LTD.

CL
GREIGHT INC.

DE
KOSUKE SHIMUTA
TOKYO JAPAN

AD
TAKESHI NAGATA

CD
TAKESHI SUZUKI

CW
TAKESHI SUZUKI

PH
TADASHI TOMONO

DM
40.6 X 28.7 IN
103 X 72.8 CM

独立したら、ひとりじゃなくなりました。

人と人が、うまくつながるためのお店です。

はじめは、一人で発足しても、仕事仲間やお客様などとのよい出逢いが、ビジネスをふくらませていくものです。私たちは印鑑、名刺、印刷、ホームページ制作代行などを通して、起業家のみなさんのおてつだいをしてきました。創業からの年、フランチャイズで全国に約300店舗を展開。これからも「安く、早く、心をこめて」、印づくりを応援します。ご相談、お問い合わせは 0120-231-8x8x まで。

〒110-0015 東京都台東区上野6-x-x 高xビルF ©くわしくは、ホームページをご覧ください。ハンコビジネスのメリットやフランチャイズのしくみ、全国の店舗案内などの情報が満載です。

制作／岡田・出田　担当／株式会社xxエイト

はんこ屋さん21
印鑑・名刺・印刷・HP制作代行

CA
CORPORATE IDENTITY

CL
NOWAKTEUFELKNYRIM

DS
HESSE DESIGN DÜSSELDORF

DE
SILKE HEIBURG
DÜSSELDORF GERMANY

AD
KLAUS HESSE

TY
UNIVERS 45 LIGHT

DM
8.3 X 11.7 IN
21 X 29.7 CM

CA
BROCHURE

DS
PH.D

CL
DICKSON'S

DE
CAROL KONO-NOBLE
SANTA MONCIA CA

AD
CLIVE PIERCY
MICHAEL HODGSON

CD
CLIVE PIERCY

CW
MIMI BEAN

TY
TRADE GOTHIC
FILOSOPHIA

DM
6.5 X 9 IN
16.5 X 22.9 CM

CA
GREETING CARDS

DS
HAEFELINGER + WAGNER
DESIGN

AD
TEAM OF HAEFELINGER +
WAGNER DESIGN
MUNICH GERMANY

CD
ANNETTE HAEFELINGER
FRANK WAGNER

TY
AKZIDENZ GROTESK BOLD
DOT MATRIX
45 HELVETICA LIGHT
OAKLAND SIX

DM
VARIOUS

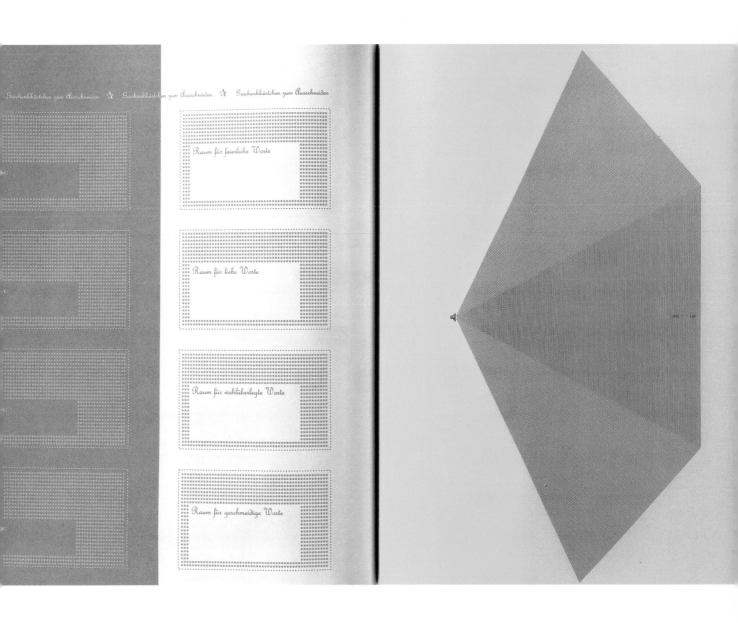

Raum für feierliche Worte

Raum für liebe Worte

Raum für wohlüberlegte Worte

Raum für geschmeidige Worte

CA
WEB SITE

DS
KARLSSONWILKER INC.

DE
HJALTI KARLSSON
JAN WILKER
NEW YORK NY

AD
HJALTI KARLSSON
JAN WILKER

CD
HJALTI KARLSSON
JAN WILKER

PG
FRANCISCO J. CASTRO

TY
TRADE GOTHIC

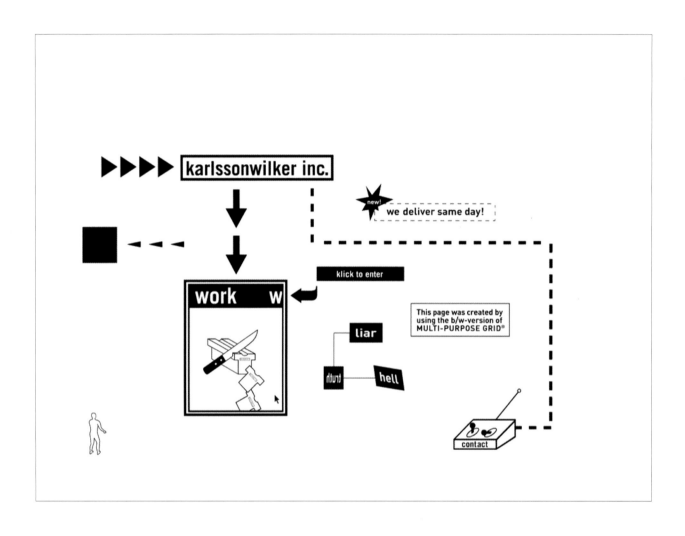

cd packaging and
tour poster for kraan,
a "psychedelic rock-
jazz cult band"
photography: eib
eibelshauser
client: kraan /
bassball records

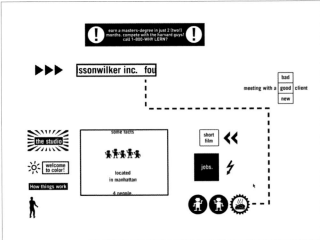

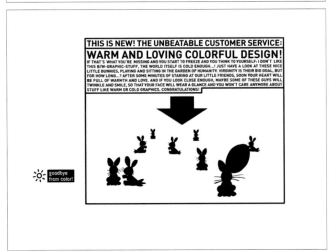

CA
MAGAZINE

DS
CAVARPAYER

CL
CDU – CENTRE FOR
DRAMA ART, ZAGREB

DE
LANA CAVAR
IRA PAYER
NARCISA VUKOJEVIĆ
ZAGREB CROATIA

IL
LANA CAVAR
NARCISA VUKOJEVIĆ

TY
UNIVERS
TRADE GOTHIC
BODONI

DM
8.7 X 10.8 IN
22 X 27.5 CM

Činjenica da je za pokretanje raznih čudnovatih strojeva u nekom performansu potrebna količina energije (a ovdje zbilja mislim na fizikalni pojam energije - ono što vam naplaćuju svakog mjeseca i mjere u kilovat-satima koju prosječno kućanstvo potroši godišnje, još uvijek ne znači da je konkretni performans energičan - on samo treba ogromnu količinu energije za postojanje. Kad za umjetničko djelo kažemo da ima energiju ili da "zrači energijom") sigurno ne mislimo na ovakve, osnovne aspekte njegova postojanja. Za krutu, fizikalnu karakterizaciju energije umjetničkog djela, promatrač nije niti potreban (kao ni umjetnost uostalom), pa je pojam energije zbilja depersonaliziran i univerzalan, ali sigurno ne odgovara istom pojmu u jeziku umjetnosti. Energičnost umjetničkog djela očigledno je vezana uz karakter percepcije promatrača. Jasno je da smo primjenjivo ovu činjenicu prihvatiti. No samu percepciju promatrača možemo promatrati s fizikalnog, preciznije rečeno mehaničkog, stanovišta pokušavajući istaknuti analogije između karaktera percepcije i osobina jednostavnih fizikalnih sistema. Percepcija gibanja tipa onda i energije gibanja u umjetničkom djelu donekle je neovisna o promatraču kad se radi o djelima koja se realiziraju i u vremenu, a ne samo u prostoru. Tako bismo npr. za jedan jedini konstantni ton kazali da ima mnogo manju kinetičku energiju od melodije. Ovdje je kinetička energija vezana očigledno uz mijenjanje strukture, oblika kroz vrijeme, gibanje. Slično je i s glumcima ili plesačima na sceni. Svako gibanje, naravno, nije isto. Tako bismo mogli reći da je gibanje (ili energija) ritmično ako se određene konfiguracije odnosno strukture, javljaju opetovano u manje-više stalnim vremenskim razmacima, analogno gibanju njihala primjerice. Problematičnije je definirati kinetičku energiju djela koja se realiziraju samo prostorno, npr. slike ili skulpture. No sama je percepcija slike proces koji traje konačno vrijeme, pa bismo kinetičku energiju slike mogli vezati uz vremensku promjenjivost njene percepcije. U stvari, jasno je da se promatrača ne možemo "riješiti". Energija umjetničkog djela vezana je kako uz aspekte umjetničkog djela koji ne ovise o promatraču, tako i uz karakter promatračeve percepcije tog djela. Potencijalnu energiju umjetničkog djela mogli bismo definirati kao energiju pohranjenu u strukturi ili strukturama tog djela. Percepcija potencijalne strukture (konfiguracije, forme) ovisit će kako o promatraču tako i o samoj strukturi.

For example, a heavy painting would contain more energy than the light one. A loud piece of music would always have more energy than a silent one. The fact that weird machines used in some performances need energy (and here I mean physical energy of the kind you pay for every month and which they measure in kilowatt hours) spent by an average family in a year, does not mean that the performance in question has artistic energy, the machines just suck up energy much in the same way a washing machine does. When we say for a piece of art that it has energy or that it "radiates energy" we surely do not think about the strict physical aspects of its existence. For a strict physical characterization of a work of art, a viewer is in fact not needed (the fact that we talk about the work of art and not a piece of paper is also of no importance at all), which makes this concept of energy in art universal. The energy of (in) the work of art is clearly related to the character of the viewer's perception of the work of art. By accepting this fact, we must abandon any hope to say something universal and widely accepted concerning the energy in art. However, the viewer's perception can be looked at in its physical (more precisely mechanical) aspect, trying to find analogies between the character of perception and the properties of more or less simple physical systems. The perception of motion (i.e. kinetic energy) in a work of art is to a point independent of the viewer when we speak about the works which exist in finite time and not only in finite space. We could say for a single constant tone that it has a much smaller kinetic energy than a melody. The kinetic energy of a work of art is clearly related to the change in structure or form through time: motion. Much the same holds concerning e.g. dancers or actors on a scene. Every kind of motion is not the same. We could say that motion (or energy) is rhythmic if particular configuration, structure repeats itself in more or less constant intervals, analogous to the motion of a pendulum for example. It is more difficult define kinetic energy of works which do not change in time and which exist only in space, such as paintings or sculptures. However, perception is a process which lasts a finite time and we could define kinetic energy of a static work of art as a temporal change of its perception. In fact, it is clear that we can not "get rid" of a viewer. The energy of the work of art is related both to the aspects of the work of art which are independent of a viewer and to the viewer's perception of the work. Potential energy of the work of art could be defined as energy stored in its structure (or structures).

Počučeo analogiju s potencijalnom energijom u fizici mogli bismo reći da potencijalnu energiju imaju strukture koje su "neravnotežne", "napete", koje se imaju tendenciju gibanjem relaksirati u ravnotežnije strukture kao što se napeta žica gitare ima tendenciju relaksirati gibanjem u svoj ravnotežni položaj čim maknemo prst s nje. Ovdje je zgodno citirati Jurija Alschitza (Lectures on "Theatre in the 21st Century") koji osim problema jezika, spomenutog u uvodu ovog članka, diskutira i pojam energije koju shvaća kao napetost (dakle, njegovo viđenje energije u kazalištu vjerojatno odgovara viđenju potencijalne energije skiciranom ovdje): "Nemamo samo probleme s različitim religijama, mi govorimo i različite jezike, različite kazališne jezike. Posjetio sam niz radionica tijekom ove konferencije i nisam razumio o čemu se raspravlja. Primijetio sam da riječ energija u stvari znači napetost." Promatrač se pojavljuje kao svojevrsni referentni nivo za mjerenje potencijalne energije slično kao što će kamen pušten s visine od 1001 m osloboditi veliku količinu svoje potencijalne energije padom u more ali samo malu količinu padom u planinsko jezero na visini od 1000 m. Mogli bismo spekulirati da se napetost strukture umjetničkog djela prenosi u napetost promatračeve neuralne mreže koja percipira djelo. Taj prijenos ovisi o stanju neuralne mreže u trenutku percepcije (što znači da je percepcija uvjetovana iskustvom, znanjem i poviješću promatrača). Slično pomanje energije umjetničkog djela (plesa) u terminima napetosti možemo naći i u iskazu Jelene Petrović (Alternative Energy, Dance, Vol 19, Issue 332, 1998): "Energija u plesu vezana je uz ideju da je prostor preuzak za ono što se zbiva, da pokret, ma kako mali bio, curi kroz vidljive granice tog prostora." Ovdje je energija vezana kako uz gibanje (kinetička energija) tako i uz napetost prostornih struktura koje to gibanje proizvodi (potencijalna energija). Gibanje i napetost strukture čine se tijesno povezanima. Slično kao i u mehanici gibanje vodi do različitih struktura (odn. promjena strukture uzrokuje gibanje) koje imaju različite potencijalne strukture, napetosti. Na kraju, svjestan sam da je proces "izvoza" pojma energije iz fizike u umjetnost koji sam skicirao u ovom članku bio vrlo osobno obojen i uvjetovan. No program definiranja pojma energije u redukcijom pojma energija na jednostavnije i vjerojatno jasnije pojmove gibanje, forma, struktura, konfiguracija i napetost.

The perception of the potential of a particular structure (configuration, form) will in general depend both on the viewer and the structure. As with potential energy in physics, for the structures which are out of equilibrium (balance), which are "tense", which have a tendency to relax through motion into more balanced structure just as a strained guitar string has a tendency to relax by oscillating around its equilibrium positions, we could say for such structures that they have potential energy. It is interesting to cite Jury Alschitz here (Lectures on "Theatre in the 21st Century") who, besides the problem of language mentioned in the introduction of this article, speaks about the concept of energy which he understands as tension (this means that his understanding of an energy in theatre probably corresponds to the notion of potential energy sketched here): "We don't just have a problem with the various 'religions', we also speak different languages, different theatre languages. I have visited a number of workshops during this conference and haven't understood what was being discussed. The use of the word 'energy', I have noticed, stands for 'tension'. The viewer appears here as a kind of a reference level for measuring the potential energy: A stone which falls from a height of 1001 m releases a large amount of its potential energy when it falls into the sea, but only a small amount when it falls into a mountain lake on a height of 1000 m. One could speculate that the tension of the structure of a work of art translates into a tension (potential energy) of viewer's neural network which perceives the work and that this translation depends on the state of the neutral network at the time of perception (this means that perception is influenced by experience, knowledge and history of the viewer). A similar understanding of energy in art (in terms of tension) can be found in an article by Jelena Petrović (Alternative Energy, Dance, Vol 19, Issue 332 (1998)): "Energy in dance has to do with the idea that space is too tight for what is going on, that the movement, however small, leaks through its visible boundaries." The energy as comprehended by J. Petrović is related both to motion (kinetic energy) and to tension of spatial structures produced by motion (potential energy). The motion and the tension of structure are tightly connected. As in mechanics, motion leads to various structures (or the change in structure leads to motion) which have different potential structures or tensions. At the end, I am aware that the process of "exporting" the concept of energy from physics into art I sketched in this article was very personally coloured. However, the program of defining a concept of energy through its reduction to simpler and clearer terms of motion, form, structure, configuration and tension was fulfilled.

CA
POSTER

CL
AMNESTY INTERNATIONAL

DS
PENTAGRAM

DE
DAISUKE ENDO
NEW YORK NY

AD
WOODY PIRTLE

TY
FRANKLIN GOTHIC

DM
33 X 27 IN
83.8 X 68.6 CM

STOP GUN TRAFFICKING

NO MORE GUNS FOR TORTURE AND HUMAN RIGHTS ABUSES

GOVERNMENTS SHOULD ADOPT AND IMPLEMENT LAWS TO PROHIBIT ARMS EXPORTS UNLESS IT CAN BE DEMONSTRATED THEY WILL NOT CONTRIBUTE TO SERIOUS HUMAN RIGHTS VIOLATIONS, CRIMES AGAINST HUMANITY OR WAR CRIMES

AMNESTY INTERNATIONAL

CA
POSTER

DS
CAHAN & ASSOCIATES

CL
AMERICAN INSTITUTE
OF GRAPHIC ARTS

DE
BOB DINETZ
SAN FRANCISCO CA

AD
BILL CAHAN
BOB DINETZ

CD
BILL CAHAN

TY
FRANKLIN GOTHIC

DM
18 X 27 IN
45.7 X 68.6 CM

CA
BOOK

DS
STRICHPUNKT

CL
PAPIERFABRIK SCHEUFELEN,
LENNINGEN

DE
CAROLINE ABELE
KIRSTEN DIETZ
TANJA GÜNTHER
FELIX WIDMAIER
GERNOT WALTER
STEPHANIE ZEHENDER
STUTTGART GERMANY

AD
KIRSTEN DIETZ
JOCHEN RÄDEKER

CD
JOCHEN RÄDEKER
KIRSTEN DIETZ

LT
KIRSTEN DIETZ

TY
RIALTO
CONDUIT
FILOSOFIA

DM
8.7 X 11.8 IN
22 X 30 CM

SIEGFRIED

EIN FAMILIENUNTERNEHMEN ZWISCHEN TAKE-OVER UND BUY-OUT

Siegfried
DIE NIBELUNGEN AG
TRAGISCH GESCHEITERTER
ÜBERNAHMEVERSUCH EINES IMPERIUMS

1 Geschäftsjahre		*4 Signet Logotype*
450		
3.3 Business-Hintergrund		
EIN FAMILIENKONZERN ZWISCHEN FEINDLICHER ÜBERNAHME UND OFFENBARUNGSEID.		

VERARBEITUNG

Papier	*Einarbeitung*	*Specials*
Scheufelen / Phoenixmotion (Kanton, 150 g/m²)	Fadenheftung, Very-Hard-Cover	**TEEBEUTEL** Lindenblütentee mit heilender Wirkung

22. Siegfried
nibelungen AG
450

seite · XX, XX

CA
STATIONERY

CL
PERIPHERE

DS
PAPRIKA COMMUNICATIONS

DE
LOUISE MAROIS
ISABELLE D'ASTOUS
MONTRÉAL CANADA

CD
LOUIS GAGNON

TY
ORATOR
UNIVERS CONDENSED

DM
VARIOUS

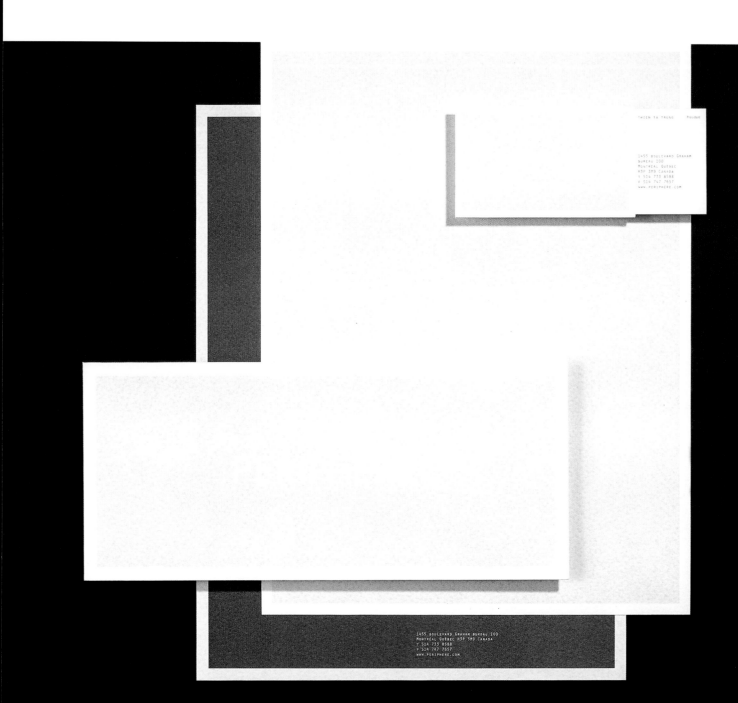

CA
BROCHURE

DS
ATELIER POISSON

DE
GIORGIO PESCE
LAUSANNE SWITZERLAND

AD
GIORGIO PESCE

CD
GIORGIO PESCE

LT
GIORGIO PESCE

PH
DANIEL BALMAT

TY
VENDÔME
FORMATA
OCR B

DM
4.5 X 3 IN
11.5 X 7.5 CM

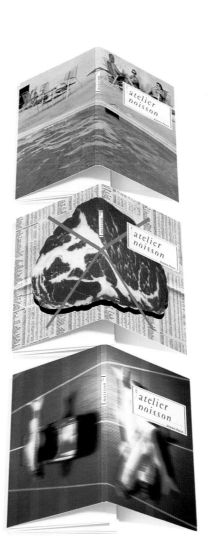

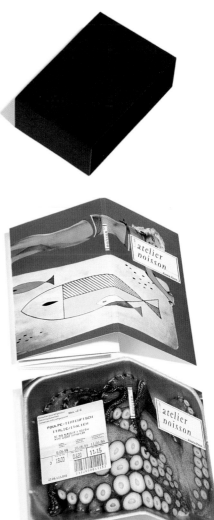

CA
STATIONERY

DS
POWELL

DE
NEIL POWELL
NEW YORK NY

TY
HANDLETTERING
FOUNDRY GRIDNICK

DM
VARIOUS

CA
PACKAGING

CL
ZING MAGAZINE AND
AESTHETICS

DE
HANS SEEGER
WAUWATOSA WI

AD
HANS SEEGER

TY
MEMPHIS EXTRA BOLD

DM
4.75 X 4.9 IN
12.1 X 12.4 CM

COMPILED

RAMMING
(or your loafer mix)

FOREST
ings

+ FUMIE
morning

TRA
older

E + VAX
go before

ICEBREAKER
melody for NATO

HOOD + DOSE ONE + WHY?
branches bare

WINDSOR FOR THE DERBY + I-SOUND
ice age blues

HIGH PRIEST + CX / KIDTRONIK
sickly

THE ETERNALS
phase 3 (of a never ending transformation)

DANIEL GIVENS
propel

33.3
playing safe. ducking kisses and getting position

ORIGINALLY COMPILED FOR THE AUTUMN 2001 ISSUE OF ZINGMAGAZINE

p.o. box 577286. chicago, il 60657   *Aesthetics*   www.aesthetics-usa.com. ast20cd.

CA
POSTER

CL
MORISAWA & COMPANY LTD.

DS
SHIMADA DESIGN OFFICE

DE
TAMOTSU SHIMADA
OSAKA JAPAN

AD
TAMOTSU SHIMADA

CW
SHINYA KAMIMURA

TY
MIDASHI MIN MA31

DM
28.7 X 40.6 IN
72.8 X 103 CM

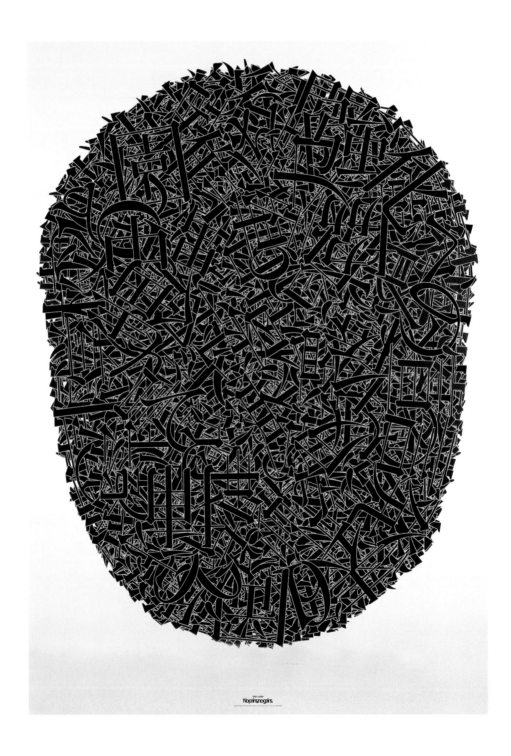

CA
LOGOTYPE

DS
AKITA DESIGN KAN INC.

CL
JAPAN ORGANIC COTTON
ASSOCIATION

DE
KAN AKITA
SHIGERU ORIHARA
TOKYO JAPAN

AD
KAN AKITA

CA
MAGAZINE COVER

CL
UNIDAD EDITORIAL, S.A.

DE
RODRIGO SÁNCHEZ
MADRID SPAIN

AD
RODRIGO SÁNCHEZ

CD
CARMELO CADEROT

TY
LETTER GOTHIC
GIZA SEVEN NINE
CLOISTER OLD STYLE

DM
7.9 X 11.25 IN
20 X 28.5 CM

EL◆MUNDO

METROPOLI

LA REVISTA DE MADRID. Nº 581. DEL 13 AL 19 DE JULIO DE 2001

Shrek,
un ogro poco convencional
de un cuento
de hadas
poco convencional
en una película de animación poco convencional

CA
MAGAZINE SPREAD

CL
ROLLING STONE

DE
KEN DELAGO
NEW YORK NY

AD
FRED WOODWARD

TY
KNOCKOUT

DM
20 X 12 IN
50.8 X 30.5 CM

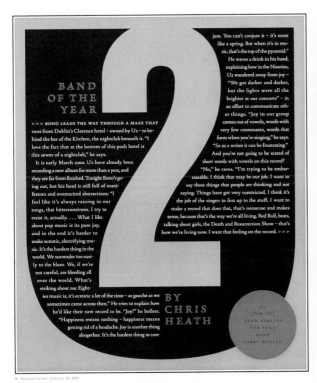

BAND OF THE YEAR

> > > BONO LEADS THE WAY THROUGH A MAZE THAT runs from Dublin's Clarence hotel – owned by U2 – to behind the bar of the Kitchen, the nightclub beneath it. "I love the fact that at the bottom of this posh hotel is this sewer of a nightclub," he says.

It is early March 2000. U2 have already been recording a new album for more than a year, and they are far from finished. Tonight Bono's going out, but his head is still full of manifestoes and overexcited abstractions: "I feel like it's always raining in our songs, that bittersweetness. I try to resist it, actually. . . . What I like about pop music is its pure joy, and in the end it's harder to make ecstatic, electrifying music. It's the hardest thing in the world. We surrender too easily to the blues. We, if we're not careful, are bleeding all over the world. What's striking about our Eighties music is, it's ecstatic a lot of the time – as gauche as we sometimes came across then." He tries to explain how he'd like their new record to be. "Joy!" he hollers. "Happiness means nothing – happiness means getting rid of a headache. Joy is another thing altogether. It's the hardest thing to con-

jure. You can't conjure it – it's more like a spring. But when it's in music, that's the top of the pyramid."

He waves a drink in his hand, explaining how in the Nineties, U2 wandered away from joy – "We got darker and darker, but the lights were all the brighter at our concerts" – in an effort to communicate other things. "Joy in our group comes out of vowels, words with very few consonants, words that form when you're singing," he says. "So as a writer it can be frustrating."

And you're not going to be scared of short words with vowels on this record?

"No," he raves. "I'm trying to be embarrassable. I think that may be our job. I want to say these things that people are thinking and not saying. Things have got very constricted. I think it's the job of the singer: to fess up to the stuff. I want to make a record that does that, that's nonsense and makes sense, because that's the way we're all living. Red Bull, beats, talking about girls, the Death and Resurrection Show – that's how we're living now. I want that feeling on the record. > > >

BY CHRIS HEATH

U2
(from left)
ADAM CLAYTON
THE EDGE
BONO
LARRY MULLEN

PHOTOGRAPHS BY MARK SELIGER

CA
POSTER

AG
HAKUHODO INC.

DS
SAITO DESIGN OFFICE

CL
HARIGAYA ELEMENTARY
SCHOOL

DE
SHIGEYUKI TAKAOKA
MAIKA SAITO
TOKYO JAPAN

AD
SHIGEYUKI TAKAOKA

CD
SHIGEYUKI TAKAOKA

LT
MASAYOSHI NAKAJO

TY
GOTHIC MB
HANDLETTERING

DM
VARIOUS

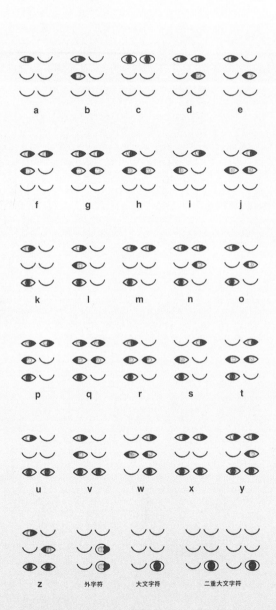

099

CA
EDITORIAL

CL
THE NEW YORK TIMES

DS
DOYLE PARTNERS

DE
STEPHEN DOYLE
NEW YORK NY

AD
PETER BUCHANAM-SMITH

PH
STEPHEN DOYLE

TY
FRANKLIN GOTHIC EXTRA
CONDENSED (WOOD)

DM
8.5 X 5.75 IN
21.6 X 14.6 CM

nidtown skyscraper, told
't shake the fear that her
ay be annihilated at any

s rules, and individuals
as best they can. Smok-
g and attendance at reli-
ces are up. And people are
ore tightly to friends and

it's up?"
. Just thought I'd give you

ver taking me to work the
aid: "Did I enjoy going to
t before the unthinkable
Of course. Big money.
the airport as a source of
ot only that. I don't like
tunnels anymore. Or over
can imagine one of these
ing splash into the water.
not good feelings for some-
profession."
ee was cold by the time I
phone. I went back to the
was planning to take an-
at Mr. Green's economic
plan when an announce-
the office loudspeaker in-
that there was a problem
velope that had shown up
nes. No one, we were told,
e the building.
began to call. What's hap-
re you all right?
. Fine.
rthing's fine, why can't you
building?
to the cafeteria and got a
of coffee.
v believed that the envelope
he Times did not contain
It was addressed to Judith
reporter who has written
ly about chemical and bio-
eapons. When Ms. Miller
ne envelope, a sweet-smel-
er, similar to baby powder,
it.
inary tests came back neg-
t even if the powder proves
— which everybody at The
d all sane people fervently
the envelope nevertheless
her wave of fear through a
ity and beyond.
: told to go about our lives as
as possible, and I can't
any better alternatives. But
York we have come up
he limits of normalcy. You
ave normally, pursuing so-
ormal activities, but there's
o escape the fact that some-
ofoundly sinister is going on.
erday's Times, in an article
ne headline "New Yorkers

Hernando de Soto is author of "The Mystery of Capital" and founder of the Institute for Liberty and Democracy in Lima, Peru.

enced mainly economic suffering, tumbling incomes and high anxiety. Those who favor the market had forgotten that the only way capitalism

ment in the 1990's by reforming laws to make it easier for the poor to gain legal title to their homes and small businesses. In my experience, the

Any campaign that does not drive a political and economic wedge between terrorists and the poor is likely to be short-lived.   □

covert action in Afghan
were those antiterrorist
ried out?
3. How many U.S., Br
sibly French command
noitering in Afghanista
have they made conta
Qaeda Afghans or Tal
tents willing to be brib
hideouts? Are comman
making deals with local
them to be part of post-
4. Has our bombing kr
Taliban broadcasting fa
the Voice of America tal
broadcast Muslim clergy
as blasphemous the sui
ers' path to paradise?
Czechs trying to run Ra
rope out of Prague?
5. What vital informa
held back from the F.B
by our Arab coalition
Did the U.S. share inte
Saudi, Egyptian and Jo
masters that comprom
Western sources in the A
6. Has Prime Ministe
secretly told President
absent absolute proof of
sein's participation in
attack — he should cour
of any move on nucle
weapons being produced
planning for "Phase II
moval of Saddam — bec
Pentagon?
7. What rule of enga
been given our special fc
ing Osama bin Laden
aides — to kill or to cap
potential benefits to us
tion outweigh the benefi
trial's world forum and
slaughter of hostages?
8. What anti-terrorist h
Saudis, Egyptians an
warned us not to ask th
what arguments are goi
the Bush administration
we have so far supinely
their demands?
9. What, if any, is the r
Baker, Brent Scowcroft
Djerijian in trying to pe
to appease "the Arab str
suring Israel to give up its
terrorism? Will bin Lad
televised embrace of the
panic the coalitionary V
into giving Hamas a terr
that would further radica
around the world?
10. What secret nego
underway with Russia to
escape of Al Qaeda le
Chechnya? We want to s
wouldn't bin Laden's pr
Vladimir Putin an excus

Stephen Doyle

Condemnation Without Absolutes

By Stanley Fish

CHICAGO

During the interval between the terrorist attacks and the United States response, a reporter called to ask me if the events of Sept. 11 meant the end of postmodernist relativism. It seemed bizarre that events so serious would be linked

the particular lived values that unite us and inform the institutions we cherish and wish to defend.

At times like these, the nation rightly falls back on the record of aspiration and accomplishment that makes up our collective understanding of what we live for. That understanding is sufficient, and far from undermining its sufficiency, postmodern thought tells us that we have grounds enough for action and justified condemnation in the democratic

better position to respond to it by taking its true measure. Making the enemy smaller than he is blinds us to the danger he presents and gives him the advantage that comes along with having been underestimated.

That is why what Edward Said has called "false universals" should be rejected: they stand in the way of useful thinking. How many times have we heard these new mantras: "We have seen the face of evil"; "these are irrational madmen":

Vladimir Putin of Russia insisted that any war against international terrorism must have as one of its objectives victory against the rebels in Chechnya.

When Reuters decided to be careful about using the word "terrorism" because, according to its news director, one man's terrorist is another man's freedom fighter, Martin Kaplan, associate dean of the Annenberg School for Communication at the University of Southern California, conti

CA
STATIONERY

DS
STUDIO/LAB

CL
PAUL F. SHOWERS,
DDS MS PC

DE
KRISTEN GURNITZ
CHICAGO IL

TY
ADOBE GARAMOND
AKZIDENZ GROTESK

DM
VARIOUS

CA
POSTER

CL
SAPPORO GRAND HOTEL

DS
TERASHIMA DESIGN CO.

DE
MASAYUKI TERASHIMA
SAPPORO JAPAN

AD
MASAYUKI TERASHIMA

LT
MASAYUKI TERASHIMA

DM
40.6 X 28.7 IN
10.3 X 72.8 CM

CA
TELEVISION TITLE

CL
DW-TV

DS
DW-TV GRAPHICS
DEPARTMENT

DE
BARBARA ORTH
BERLIN GERMANY

AD
BARBARA ORTH

CD
HOLGER ZEH

TY
HOEFLER TEXT
ITC AVANT GARDE GOTHIC
ITC AMERICAN TYPEWRITER

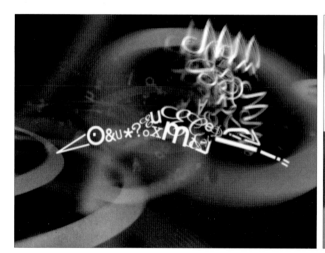

CA
CATALOG

CL
PHOTONICA AKA

DS
TOLLESON DESIGN

DE
STEVE TOLLESON
CRAIG CLARK
SAN FRANCISCO CA

AD
STEVE TOLLESON

TY
TRADE GOTHIC EXTENDED
REMINGTON PLAIN
ARISTON

DM
6 X 9 IN
15.2 X 22.9 CM

CA
STATIONERY

DS
HEINE/LENZ/ZIZKA

DE
ACHIM HEINE
MICHAEL LENZ
SONIA RECK
PETER ZIZKA
FRANKFURT GERMANY

TY
LETTER GOTHIC
STANDARD PUNCH

DM
VARIOUS

HEINE/LENZ/ZIZKA

MEF.030 Art Frankfurt 2002, Feindaten

17.05.2001
Heine/Lenz/Zizka Projekte GmbH, Frankfurt/Berlin

HEINE/LENZ/ZIZKA

Leica Camera AG
Hanns-Peter Cohn
Oskar-Barnack-Straße 11
D-35606 Solms

HEINE/LENZ/ZIZKA

Michael David Ochs, Design

Heine/Lenz/Zizka Projekte GmbH, Frankfurt/Berlin
Niddastraße 84, 60329 Frankfurt, www.heine-lenz-zizka.com
Telefon 069-24 24 24-0, Telefax 069-24 24 24-99
m.ochs@heine-lenz-zizka.com

106

CA
POSTER

DS
DOYLE PARTNERS

CL
ART DIRECTORS CLUB

DE
STEPHEN DOYLE
NEW YORK NY

CD
STEPHEN DOYLE

PH
VICTOR SCHRAGER

TY
SABON

DM
19 X 30 IN
48.3 X 76.2 CM

107

CA
BOOK

DS
+ROSEBUD

DE
ENRICO BRAVI
(URBINO ITALY)
KURT CORNELIS
(ANTWERP BELGIUM)
DISPLAY
(LUZERN SWITZERLAND)
HUGO FEISTHAMEL
(VIENNA AUSTRIA)
SILJA GÖTZ (MADRID SPAIN)
ULF HARR (VIENNA AUSTRIA)
FRITZ T. MAGISTRIS
(VIENNA AUSTRIA)
MASHICA (MADRID SPAIN)

RAPHAEL MUNTWYLER
(LUZERN SWITZERLAND)
LISA PRICHARD
(LOS ANGELES CA)
AXEL PRICHARD-
SCHMITZBERGER
(LOS ANGELES CA)
TIMO REGER
(NUREMBERG GERMANY)

AD
KATJA FÖSSEL
COLOGNE GERMANY
RALF HERMS
VIENNA AUSTRIA

CD
RALF HERMS

TY
DTL ALBERTINA
ZURICH

DM
6.7 X 9.6 IN
17 X 24.5 CM

Das ist der Text für ein Buchcover. **Vorerst steht hier noch ein beliebiger und nichtssagender Text. Ein Text** der in der richtigen grafischen Auf**bereitung ausschliesslich dazu dient, den Titel dieses Buches aussagekräftig zu machen. Selbstverständlich ist die hier abgebildete Zeichenkette nur dazu geeignet, einen allgemeinen visuellen Eindruck zu vermitteln. Der tatsächliche Inhalt ist** in diesem **Moment noch völlig nebensächlich. Der Betrachter** soll den Text ja gar nicht **lesen um nicht von der äusseren Form abgele**nkt zu werden. Dieser Text **wird in dieser Form natürlich nie in Druck g**ehen. Später wird er allerdings sehr aus**führlich über das Thema un**d die Inhalte dieses Buches **informieren. Vorerst kommt ihm jedoch nu**r eine reine Platzhalterfunktion **zu, obgleich Schriftart, Schriftgrösse, Zeilenabstand und Laufweite bereits einen verbindlichen Eindruck über das Erscheinungsbild vermitteln sollen. Nur so kann das Cover unter rein form**alen Gesichtspunkten objektiv **beurteilt werden. Dies ist insbesonde**re bei einem **Designbuch von grosser Bedeutung, d**a **hier** der Gestaltung des Titels eine wichtige **Rolle bei der Kaufentscheidung z**ukommt. This **text is for the cover of a** book. **At the moment, it is just ran**dom meaningless text. It is text **that serves to emphasize the title of th**is publication by being placed **in its formal graphical context. Of course** the chain of symbols depicted **here is** only **employed to convey a visual** impression. **The** actual contents **are to**tally **irrelevant at the moment. The** reader isn't even supposed **to read the** text to **insure that it doesn't distract** him from the form. Of course this

"One of the most arresting, insightful and scandalous books in recent memory…"
MARKETING MANAGER

"A publishing milestone."
PRODUCTION COORDINATOR

"This is the book I wish I had written."
INTERN

"The one book on Blindtext I'd have if I could have just one. A classic."
EDITOR-IN-CHIEF

CA
BROCHURE

CL
APPLIED MATERIALS

DS
JACOBS FULTON DESIGN
GROUP

DE
GEOFF AHMANN
PALO ALTO CA

AD
GEOFF AHMANN

PH
MICHAEL WILSON

TY
BEMBO

DM
6.25 X 8.5 IN
15.9 X 21.6 CM

CA
WEB SITE

CL
PETER LEVERMAN

DS
CONCRETE DESIGN
COMMUNICATIONS INC.

DE
CLAIRE DAWSON
TORONTO CANADA

AD
JOHN PYLYCZAK
DITI KATONA

PG
DAMIAN DE SHANE-GILL

TY
KNOCKOUT

111

112

CA
ADVERTISEMENT

AG
DENTSU INC.

DS
AD BRAIN

CL
WORLD VISION JAPAN

DE
EMIKO ORITA
TOKYO JAPAN

AD
TAKASHI FUKUI

CD
TAKASHI FUKUI
MIYAKO MAEKITA

CW
MIYAKO MAEKITA

TY
MB101

DM
28.7 X 40.6 IN
72.8 X 103 CM

CA
ADVERTISEMENT

CL
INTEGRALIS

DS
STORM STRATEGIC

DE
SPENCER BUCK
ALEX BANE
BRADFORD ON AVON
ENGLAND

AD
ALEX BANE

CD
SPENCER BUCK

LT
SPENCER BUCK

TY
TIMES NEW ROMAN
(MODIFIED)

DM
8.25 X 11.75 IN
21 X 29.7 CM

Our clients include:

If your
business
is our business
it won't be
anyone else's

Impressed? You would be ...if we could name them. We can't, because to them, security is paramount. That's why they use Integralis, Europe's leader in IT and e-commerce security services and products. Our clients include 50 of the FTSE 100 and 20 of the DAX 30 companies. They know their secrets are safe with us. Integralis – *the best kept secret.*

AUSTRIA   CZECH REPUBLIC   FRANCE   GERMANY   SWITZERLAND   UNITED KINGDOM   USA

Your secrets are safe with us. Integralis is Europe's independent leader in IT and e-commerce security. We identify and analyse your requirements, then offer solutions to fit your company. Our range of Managed Services makes high quality Internet security simple and painless. Now that's something to shout about. Integralis – *the best kept secret.*

INTEGRALIS
www.integralis.com

AUSTRIA   CZECH REPUBLIC   FRANCE   GERMANY   SWITZERLAND   UNITED KINGDOM   USA

CA
MAIN TITLE

DS
DESIGN BOUTIQUE

CL
PARAMOUNT PICTURES

DE
KEITH PANG
HOLLYWOOD CA

AD
GARSON YU

CD
GARSON YU

IA
TODD MESHER

TY
MINION REGULAR

115

CA
EXHIBITION BOOTH
INSTALLATION

AG
KMS GERMANY

DS
MEDIADESIGNCOMPANY

CL
VIAG

DE
THOMAS WERNBACHER
MUNICH GERMANY

AD
ARND BUSS VON KUK

CD
LUIS CASTRILLO

LT
THOMAS WERNBACHER
LUIS CASTRILLO

MS
ANDREAS LIST/TTM
PRODUKTION

TY
MYRIAD

CA
BUSINESS CARD

CL
PATTI KATCHA, SEAMSTRESS

DS
JENNIFER KATCHA,
FREELANCE DESIGN

DE
JENNIFER L. KATCHA
MADISON WI

AD
JENNIFER L. KATCHA

PT
MIKE SHEAHEN, FIRECAST
LETTERPRESS

TY
FILOSOFIA
FOUND TYPE

DM
2 X 3.5 IN
5.1 X 8.9 CM

CA
BOOK COVER

CL
DOUBLEDAY CANADA

DS
PYLON DESIGN INC.

DE
KEVIN HOCH
TORONTO CANADA

AD
KEVIN HOCH
SCOTT CHRISTIE

CD
SCOTT CHRISTIE

TY
BEMBO

DM
4.5 X 7.5 IN
11.3 X 19.1 CM

evelyn lau

evelyn lau

my writing—helped me be a better writer, helped me publish and live my life as a writer—I would never ask him for anything else. The rest of my life could dissolve into heartbreaks and catastrophes, into a litany of losses, but as long as he made sure I was still writing and publishing, then he was doing his job and I had no right to ask him for help in any other area.

As a child I thought ... such a duty, and I still remember the shock I felt reading about an author's ... in the newspaper, the unfinished book they had left behind. If they were working on a manuscript, how could they succumb to mortal illness and accident? It was their duty to finish that book, it was why they were here on this earth; they were no more than vehicles for that story, and their God should see that they lived—however miserably—to carry out their work. I believed as long as I was working on a poem, a story, a book—over two summers, when I was nine and ten, I wrote two full-length novels, long lost—I could not die. It is only now, looking back, that I think I must have been aware of my mortality and afraid of it, and that this was a way of dealing with that fear. I remember walking dreamily

INSIDE OUT

Doubleday
Canada

CA
MAGAZINE

DS
THE BANG

CL
COUPE

DE
BILL DOUGLAS
TORONTO CANADA

AD
BILL DOUGLAS

TY
ZURICH
JUDAS

DM
9.6 X 11.5 IN
24.5 X 29.2 CM

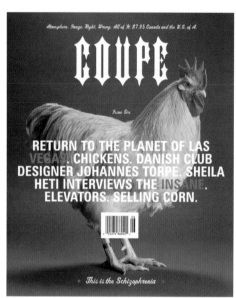

CA
BOOK

PB
LITTLE BROWN
AND COMPANY

DE
CAROL HAYES
NEW YORK NY

TY
CLARENDON
SHOWBOAT
TOUSSANT

DM
5.6 X 8.5 IN
14.2 X 21.6 CM

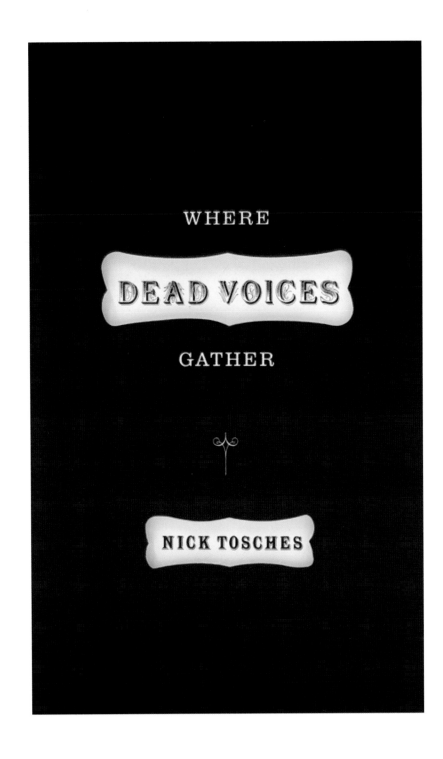

CA
PACKAGING

DS
MARTHA STEWART LIVING
OMNIMEDIA, INC.

DE
DONALD WEST
NEW YORK NY

AD
DONALD WEST

CD
ANDREW GRAY

TY
MSLGOTHIC BOLD

DM
12.5 X 10.5 IN
31.8 X 26.8 CM

CA
BROCHURE

DS
METHODOLOGIE

DE
MINH NGUYEN
SEATTLE WA

TY
NEWS GOTHIC

DM
VARIOUS

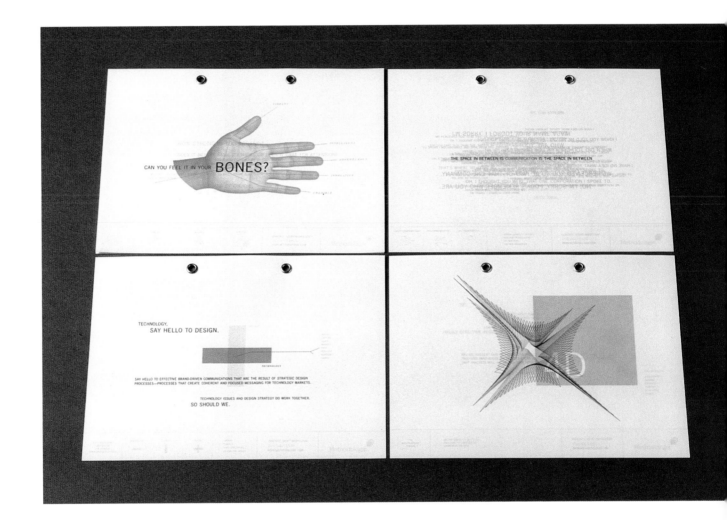

CA
BROCHURE

CL
FRIEND AND JOHNSON

DS
PH.D

DE
CLIVE PIERCY
SANTA MONICA CA

AD
CLIVE PIERCY
MICHAEL HODGSON

CD
CLIVE PIERCY

TY
AKZIDENZ GROTESK

DM
11 X 7 IN
27.9 X 17.8 CM

friend and johnson photography and illustration volume eight

eight/inspired.
ANN FIELD: brancusi, bird, hermes squares, chappie. danny kaye movies, matisse, jean-michel frank and a very tall designer. BILL PHELPS: eyes, wheels, strand, silence.... fallingwater, shifting sands, zuzu's petals and the isle of man tt. HANNES SCHMID: wenders, eno, harleys, helmut lang. madonna, plastic, polke and sushi. PAUL WEARING: the specials, chihuly, marvin gaye, gehry. vic and bob, miles davis, selmer saxophones and my life as a dog. SCOGIN MAYO: koolhaus, bauhaus, early bowie, late nights, pawson, jill, jungle and doctor no. JOCK McDONALD: russians, cubans, eccentrics, eskimos, surfers, japanese, elvis impersonators and everything in between. GISELLE POTTER: pee-wee herman, cirque du soleil, roald dahl, mr. ed. tim burton, beatrix potter, harry potter and scout in to kill a mockingbird. GEOF KERN: jacques tati, marcel broodthaers, outerbridge, buster keaton, tom and jerry, the stones, guy bourdin and vermeer. JAMES NOEL SMITH: newspapers, riesling kabinett, afternoon naps and tennessee. pick-ups, chainsaws, lawrence of arabia and dostoyevski. TIM SIMMONS: the man from u.n.c.l.e., bangers and mash, bang—

CA
PACKAGING

DS
SAGMEISTER INC.

CL
BLUE Q

DE
STEFAN SAGMEISTER
HJALTI KARLSSON
NEW YORK NY

AD
STEFAN SAGMEISTER

CD
STEFAN SAGMEISTER

CW
KAREN SALMANSOHN

LT
HJALTI KARLSSON

TY
NEWS GOTHIC

DM
4.75 X 6.5 IN
12.1 X 16.5 CM

CA
POSTER

CL
PORTFOLIO CENTER

DE
JAMES VICTORE
BEACON NY

TY
BERTHOLD HELVETICA
ADOBE CASLON

DM
23.5 X 16.5 IN
59.7 X 41.9 CM

CA
POSTER

CL
DESIGN INDABA

DS
FROST DESIGN

DE
VINCE FROST
LONDON ENGLAND

AD
VINCE FROST

CD
VINCE FROST

TY
FRANKLIN GOTHIC
CONDENSED

DM
60 X 40 IN
152.4 X 101.6 CM

David Carson has cancelled
yet another event at the last minute
Luckily Vince Frost has stepped
in to save the day

David Carson

Vince Frost, Frost Design, London

Design Indaba Workshop Series 2
3rd Floor, Design Building,
Cape Technikon
26 October

Kindly sponsored by

Cape Metropolitan Tourism
Uthingo
Sappi
Creda
Interactive Africa

A Frosty day in Cape Town

CA
CORPORATE IDENTITY

DS
THE VALENTINE GROUP

CL
HELEN NORMAN

DE
ROBERT VALENTINE
DAVID MEREDITH
NEW YORK NY

CD
ROBERT VALENTINE

TY
TRADE GOTHIC EXTENDED
TRADE GOTHIC

DM
8.5 X 11 IN
21.6 X 27.9 CM

HELEN NORMAN

H

HELEN NORMAN

2950 GARRETT ROAD
WHITEHALL MD 21161

HELEN NORMAN

CA
ANNUAL REPORT

CL
4MBO INTERNATIONAL
ELECTRONIC AG

DS
STRICHPUNKT

DE
KIRSTEN DIETZ
STUTTGART GERMANY

AD
KIRSTEN DIETZ

CD
JOCHEN RÄDEKER

LT
KIRSTEN DIETZ

PH
KAI LOGES
ANDREAS LANGEN

TY
RIALTO
TRADE GOTHIC

DM
8.3 X 10.2 IN
21 X 26 CM

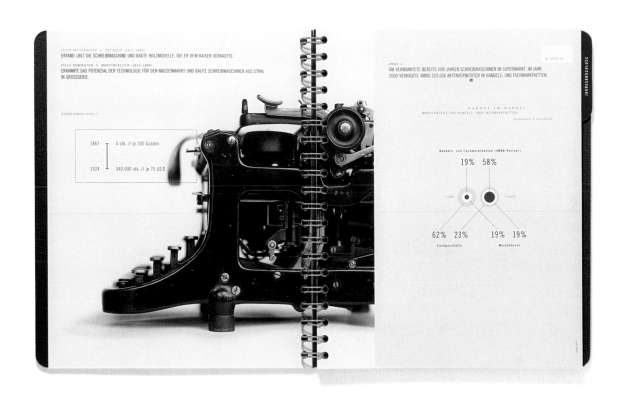

128

CA
STATIONERY

AG
LIQUID AGENTUR FÜR
GESTALTUNG

CL
SILKE MARSEN

DE
CARINA ORSCHULKO
ILJA SALLACZ
AUGSBURG GERMANY

TY
EUROSTILE

DM
28.25 X 11.7 IN
21 X 29.7 CM

CA
MAGAZINE SPREAD

CL
ROLLING STONE

DE
SIUNG TJIA
NEW YORK NY

AD
FRED WOODWARD

TY
AGENCY

DM
20 X 12 IN
50.8 X 30.5 CM

CA
BOOK

CL
ARTISAN (WORKMAN
PUBLISHING COMPANY)

DS
DOYLE PARTNERS

DE
VIVIAN GHAZARIAN
NEW YORK NY

CD
STEPHEN DOYLE

PH
MARIA ROBLEDO

TY
HFT CHAMPION GOTHIC
CORPORATE
SABON

DM
7.1 X 9.6 IN
18 X 24.3 CM

CA
CALENDAR

DS
TERASHIMA DESIGN CO.

CL
ALEPH INC.

DE
MASAYUKI TERASHIMA
SAPPORO JAPAN

AD
MASAYUKI TERASHIMA

TY
FUTURA LIGHT

DM
7.2 X 10.1 IN
18.2 X 25.7 CM

132

CA
ADVERTISEMENT

DS
MOTION THEORY

CL
SHOWTIME NETWORKS

DE
MATHEW CULLEN
KAAN ATILLA
VENICE CA

AD
MATHEW CULLEN

CD
CHRISTINA BLACK
CARRIE HIRSCH
MATHEW CULLEN

ED
MARK HOFFMAN

TY
TRADE GOTHIC

CA
CORPORATE IDENTITY

CL
MARKUS FRIEDRICH
RUSSLER

DS
AGENTUR 42

DE
MARIO FUHR
MAINZ GERMANY

AD
MARIO FUHR

TY
CENTENNIAL

DM
VARIOUS

Markus Friedrich Russler, der;
-, (*Küsterhaus*)...Kirchgasse 13;
[D-65396] → Walluf am Rhein;
([*Tele*]fon 0 61 23.97 24 25; ...fax
97 24 26)

Markus Friedrich Russler, der;
-, (*Küsterhaus*)...Kirchgasse 13;
[D-65396] → Walluf am Rhein;

 Mit freundlicher Empfehlung

Markus Friedrich Russler, der;
-, (*Küsterhaus*)...Kirchgasse 13;
[D-65396] → Walluf am Rhein;
([*Tele*]fon 0 61 23.97 24 25; ...fax
97 24 26)

Markus Friedrich Russler, der;
-, (*Küsterhaus*)...Kirchgasse 13;
[D-65396] → Walluf am Rhein;
([*Tele*]fon 0 61 23.97 24 25; ...fax
97 24 26)

CA
BOOK COVER

DS
PYLON DESIGN INC.

CL
RANDOM HOUSE OF
CANADA LTD.

DE
GARY CLEMENT
SCOTT CHRISTIE
TORONTO CANADA

CD
SCOTT CHRISTIE

TD
GARY CLEMENT

TY
HANDLETTERING

DM
8.5 X 5.75 IN
21.6 X 14.6 CM

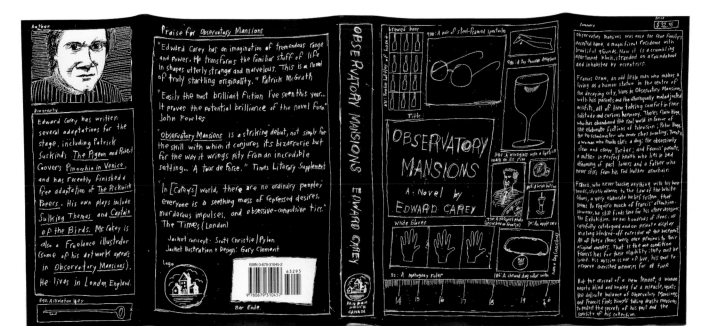

CA
TITLE/ADVERTISEMENT

DS
BLIND

CL
NISSAN

AG
TBWA/CHIAT/DAY

DE
VANESSA MARZAROLI
LAWRENCE WYATT
SANTA MONICA CA

CD
VANESSA MARZAROLI
CHRIS DO

3D
LAWRENCE WYATT

2D
DAVID KERMAN

FL
LAWRENCE WYATT

EP
ELIZABETH HUMMER

PD
AMANDA LEHMAN

ED
ERIK BUTH

TY
BETA SANS
CUSTOM

CA
PACKAGING

CL
CONSOLE/PAYOLA

DS
FACTOR PRODUCT

DE
STEFAN BOGNER
MUNICH GERMANY

AD
STEFAN BOGNER
AXEL SCHILDT

CD
STEFAN BOGNER

TY
ITC AVANT GARDE GOTHIC
HELVETICA ROUNDED

DM
VARIOUS

CA
BOOK

CL
KEITH CARTER

DS
PENTAGRAM

DE
D. J. STOUT
NANCY MCMILLEN
AUSTIN TX

AD
D. J. STOUT

TY
HELVETICA

DM
11.25 X 11.25 IN
28.6 X 28.6 CM

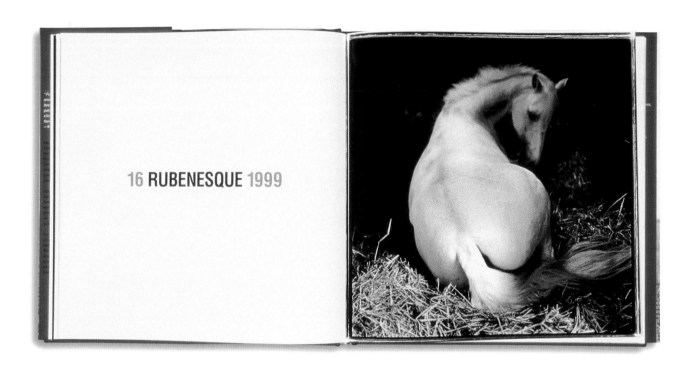

CA
CALENDAR

DS
ATELIER BEINERT

AG
WWW.ATELIER-BEINERT.DE

CL
ARCHIV VERLAG WERNER,
MUNICH

DE
WOLFGANG BEINERT
MUNICH GERMANY

AD
WOLFGANG BEINERT

CD
WOLFGANG BEINERT

CY
WOLFGANG BEINERT

TY
CONCORDE NOVA
SABBATH BLACK BOLD
BASE 9

DM
11.7 X 16.5 IN
29.7 X 42 CM

CA
POSTER

DS
MILTON GLASER, INC.

CL
SCHOOL OF VISUAL ARTS

DE
MILTON GLASER
NEW YORK NY

AD
SILAS RHODES

TY
AMERICAN TYPEWRITER

DM
30 X 45.5 IN
76.2 X 115.6 CM

I ♥
NY
MORE
THAN
EVER

School of VISUAL ARTS

CA
POSTER

CL
JAZZ IN WILLISAU

DS
NIKLAUS TROXLER DESIGN

DE
NIKLAUS TROXLER
WILLISAU SWITZERLAND

AD
NIKLAUS TROXLER

TY
CHICAGO

DM
35.6 X 50.4 IN
90.5 X 128 CM

CA
ANNUAL REPORT

CL
iSTAR FINANCIAL INC.

AG
ADDISON

DE
CHRISTINA EFTHIMIA
ANTONOPOULOS
NEW YORK NY

CD
RICHARD COLBOURNE

PH
NIGEL PARRY

TY
FRUTIGER
MRS. EAVES

DM
9 X 11 IN
22.7 X 27.9 CM

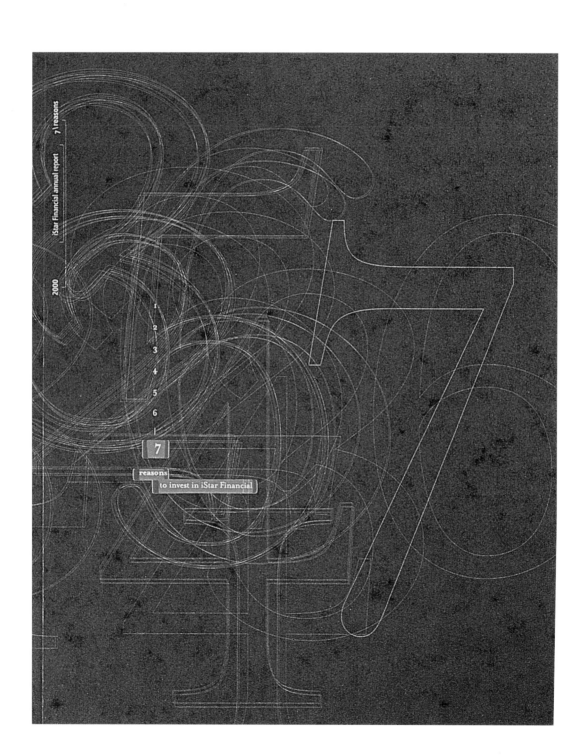

143

CA
LOGOTYPE

DS
PENTAGRAM

CL
PORT AUTHORITY OF NEW
YORK AND NEW JERSEY

DE
MICHAEL GERICKE
LIOR VATURI
NEW YORK NY

TY
HELVETICA
NEUE LIGHT

CA
BOOK COVER

DS
RIGSBY DESIGN

CL
GRAPHIS INTERNATIONAL
PRESS

DE
PAMELA ZUCCKER
HOUSTON TX

AD
LANA RIGSBY

CD
LANA RIGSBY

CY
PAMELA ZUCCKER

TY
HAND DRAWN
(BASED ON MASON)

DM
8.9 X 12 IN
19.4 X 30.5 CM

CA
BROCHURE

CL
BUSINESS PLANNING
SYSTEMS

DS
TANAGRAM

DE
GRANT DAVIS
CHICAGO IL

AD
GRANT DAVIS

CW
TODD LIEF

IL
KEVIN SPROULS
SWEETWATER NJ

TY
BELIZIO

DM
8 X 11 IN
20.3 X 27.9 CM

CA
BROCHURE

CL
UNIVERSITY OF SOUTHERN
CALIFORNIA

DE
KAREN BERNDT
ANITA LUU
SAN FRANCISCO CA

AD
KIT HINRICHS

CD
KIT HINRICHS

DS
PENTAGRAM

IL
GARY BASEMAN
JOHN CRAIG
JOHN CUNEO
REGAN DUNNICK
JEFF FISHER
JANICE LOWRY
WILL NELSON
GARY OVERACRE
CHRIS PAYNE
MERLE REAGLE
REINECK & REINECK
ANTHONY RUSSO
GORDON STUDER
JEFF WEST
MICK WIGGINS
PHILLIPE WEISBECKER

PH
GERALD BYBEE
JEFF CORWIN
BOB ESPARZA
STEVEN HELLER
ROBERT LANDAU
JOHN LIVZEY
BARRY ROBINSON
PATRICIA TRYFOROS
BILL VARIE

TY
NEWS GOTHIC
BODONI

DM
11 X 14 IN
27.9 X 35.6 CM

CA
LOGOTYPE/TITLE

DS
3007

CL
AUSTRIAN CULTURAL
FORUMS

DE
JOCHEN FILL
ULF HARR
CORINNA RÖDEL
VIENNA AUSTRIA

AD
EVA DRANAZ
JOCHEN FILL

PD
JOCHEN FILL

TY
ZURICH BOLD CONDENSED

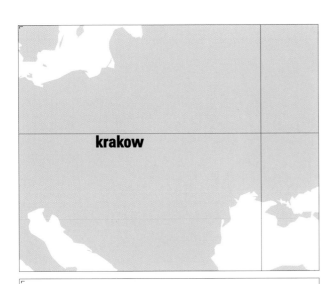

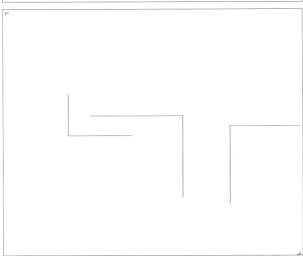

CA
BROCHURE

CL
APPLIED MATERIALS

DS
JACOBS FULTON DESIGN
GROUP

DE
GEOFF AHMANN
PALO ALTO CA

AD
GEOFF AHMANN

PH
MICHAEL WILSON

TY
BEMBO

DM
6.25 X 8.5 IN
15.9 X 21.6 CM

CA
POSTER

DS
GIFFHORN UND SERRES
DESIGN

DE
HOLGER GIFFHORN
WUPPERTAL GERMANY
THOMAS SERRES
NORDRHEIN-WESTFALEN
GERMANY

AD
HOLGER GIFFHORN
THOMAS SERRES

CD
HOLGER GIFFHORN
THOMAS SERRES

LT
HOLGER GIFFHORN

TY
UNIVERS 57 CONDENSED

DM
23.4 X 33.1 IN
59.4 X 84.1 CM

CA
BROCHURE

CL
MOHAWK PAPER MILLS

DS
HOWRY DESIGN ASSOCIATES

DE
TY WHITTINGTON
SAN FRANCISCO CA

AD
JILL HOWRY

TY
HELVETICA

DM
11 X 17 IN
27.9 X 43.2 CM

CA
MAGAZINE

DS
PENTAGRAM

CL
LA FABRICA
MADRID SPAIN

DE
CAROLINA NÚÑEZ
LAIA ROSÉS
LONDON ENGLAND

AD
FERNANDO GUTIÉRREZ

CD
FERNANDO GUTIÉRREZ

TY
JOANNA

DM
11.8 X 15.75 IN
30 X 40 CM

CA
CORPORATE IDENTITY

CL
POLAR MUSIC PRIZE

DS
HAPPY FORSMAN &
BODENFORS

DE
GAVIN SMART
GOTHENBURG SWEDEN

AD
LOUISE LINDGREN

CD
ANDERS KORNESTEDT

IL
FREDRIK PERSSON

TY
TRADE GOTHIC

DM
VARIOUS

POLAR MUSIC PRIZE

THE ROYAL SWEDISH ACADEMY OF MUSIC AWARD

CA
BOOK

DS
RE:DESIGN

CL
ALBIN O. KUHN LIBRARY
GALLERY

DE
MARGARET RE
SILVER SPRING MD

AD
MARGARET RE

CD
MARGARET RE

PH
PEGGY FOX
BALTIMORE MD

CT
CYNTHIA WAYNE
ALBIN O. KUHN LIBRARY
GALLERY UMBC

TY
SCALA
SCALA SANS

DM
8 X 9 IN
20.3 X 22.9 CM

Patapsco Portrait of a Valley

8 · 9

pf I trained as a painter, which provided the background in and acclimation towards the fine arts. I started a family and never got an undergraduate degree and am largely self-taught. The first documentary project I ever worked on was with Tom Beck from UMBC's Albin O. Kuhn Library and the Equitable Photographic Survey of Maryland in 1979. I was sent down to southern Maryland in St. Mary's County. I photographed the fishermen and oyster tongers and the tobacco farmers and the Amish. Also the test pilots at the Patuxent Naval Airbase and an elderly politician named Buck Briscoe. So I learned a lot about working on my own from that project. Also my commercial work has included a lot of photography for brochures for schools and institution, for which I would have to make a picture story out of the place and people. In some situations, I work without any kind of direction, and other situations can be very highly structured. This work has allowed me to use both approaches, and taught me to work quickly and to be able to visualize the story around it. I must say, this is the only project where I was given only one roll of film per subject, so that made it sort of a zen thing. ○

Franklin *"We had a little men's chorus. It was called Gaines' Men's Chorus. We got around pretty good... We went—it seemed a long distance—we went to Brooklyn, New York..."*

William *"See, it was three Cagers and two Fields... We didn't go out to get paid. We just sang, you know? Somebody might give a little something, but the bulk of what we got, it went to the piano player..."*

cw Let's talk about the personal and professional experiences which influenced each of you, and which brought you to this project and to this point in your careers.

ak I have a Master's degree in folklore from Memorial University of Newfoundland and Labrador. I guess the first and most influential project for me was the oral history I did while I was still in graduate school. It was an oral history of the Eastern European Jews who settled in St. John's, in Newfoundland, and I went after the story as my thesis topic. I was then asked by the university press if I wanted to perform surgery on the thesis and turn it into a book, which I did happily. And a year after the book came out, I co-produced a radio documentary for the CBC using material from those taped interviews with the immigrants and their children.

Later I did a folklife survey of Beaufort County in North Carolina for the North Carolina Arts Council, and I did a survey of traditional artists among the immigrant and refugee communities in Northern Virginia for the Virginia Foundation for the Humanities. I've also worked as a travel writer for National Geographic publications and have spent months on the road sensing stories out of places. That has been

Franklin *"Yeah, it was all spiritual—but it was southern style... We had got to the point that, even if they say would be Gaines' Male Singers in church, everybody'd be clapping 'cause they know they was going to hear some good sounds."*

William *"See, all three of us, we looked alike. We all had gray hair...we was all dressed alike.... And we'd rock up the church—we'd rock the church up now! And wherever we went, we could go back again."*

Franklin 'Scrammy' Cager,
age 87 and William Cager, age 75
Truck Drivers
ELKRIDGE

tremendous training. So has my background in American literature which has given me an appreciation for language and the vernacular—which is one thing I love about oral history. To go back to your question, what influence did those projects have on this project, it's really a question of experience—learning about my role in the interviewing process, learning more about people, learning more about equipment... losing that sense of self-consciousness. I think an important element in all these projects for me is that I've been an outsider

in all of these communities. And I've learned that there's an advantage to being an outsider because people want to teach you, they don't make assumptions about what you know and want to give you the whole story. If someone is being interviewed by another member of the community, there's a tendency to gloss over details and background which doesn't make for great narrative. And this is really all about story. As they say, the story is everything. And that's what we go for, those of us who are doing this kind of work. ○

Franklin "Scrammy" Cager
1999-2000
Gelatin silver print
7 ¹/₂" x 11 ¹/₂"

CA
POSTER

DS
APELOIG DESIGN

CL
CITÉ DU LIVRE
FÊTE DU LIVRE
AIX EN PROVENCE

DE
PHILIPPE APELOIG
PARIS FRANCE

AD
PHILIPPE APELOIG

CD
PHILIPPE APELOIG

TY
AKZIDENZ GROTESK

DM
45 X 69 IN
114.3 X 175.3 CM

CA
CORPORATE IDENTITY

CL
PORTLAND ADVERTISING
FEDERATION

DS
SANDSTROM DESIGN

DE
STEVE SANDSTROM
PORTLAND OR

AD
STEVE SANDSTROM

CD
STEVE SANDSTROM

CW
GREG EIDEN
STEVE SANDSTROM

TY
FRANKLIN GOTHIC
CENTURY SCHOOLBOOK

DM
VARIOUS

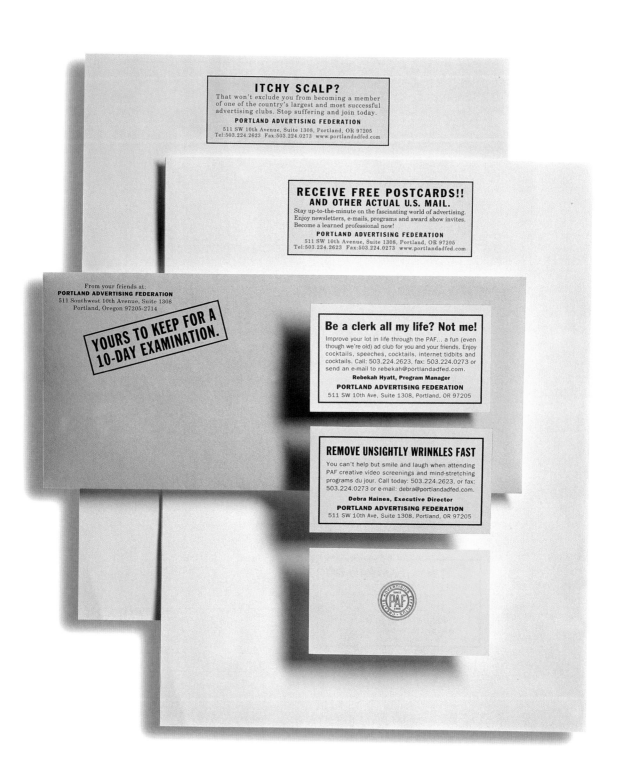

CA
CATALOG

DS
FROETER DESIGN
COMPANY INC.

CL
THE SMART MUSEUM OF ART

DE
TOM ZURAWSKI
CHICAGO IL

CD
CHRIS FROETER

LT
H. C. WESTERMANN

TY
ADOBE GARAMOND

DM
9 X 12 IN
22.9 X 30.5 CM

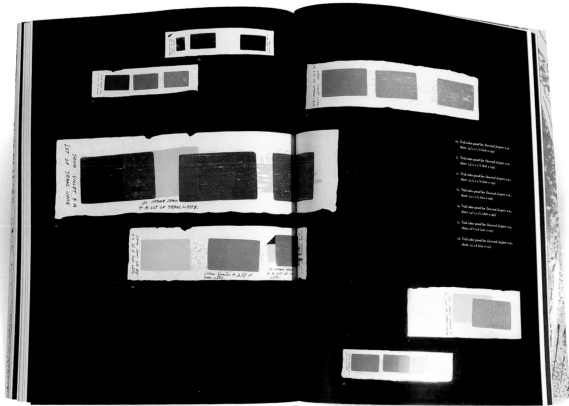

CA
ADVERTISEMENT

AG
SAATCHI & SAATCHI
NEW ZEALAND

CL
SECONDARY PRINCIPALS
ASSOCIATION OF NEW
ZEALAND (SPANZ)

DE
LEN CHEESEMAN
WELLINGTON NEW ZEALAND

AD
MAGGIE MOUAT
EUGENE RUANE
LEN CHEESEMAN

CD
GAVIN BRADLEY

AM
JASON BOWDEN

TY
FRANKLIN GOTHIC WIDE

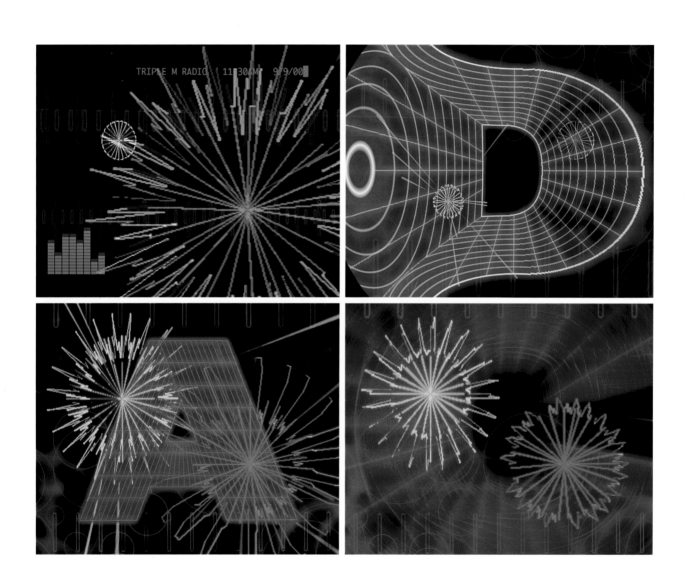

CA
POSTER

CL
MUSEUM OF MODERN ART
TOYAMA

DS
FONS M. HICKMANN

DE
FONS M. HICKMANN
BERLIN GERMANY

AD
FONS M. HICKMANN

TY
CORPORATE

DM
47.2 X 33.1 IN
120 X 84 CM

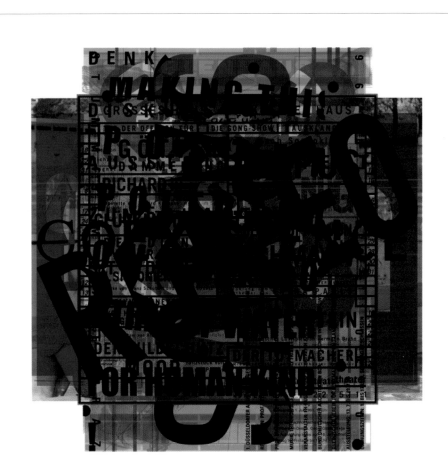

160

CA
POSTER

CL
JAZZ IN WILLISAU

DS
NIKLAUS TROXLER DESIGN

DE
NIKLAUS TROXLER
WILLISAU SWITZERLAND

AD
NIKLAUS TROXLER

TY
FUTURA BOLD

DM
35.6 X 50.4 IN
90.5 X 128 CM

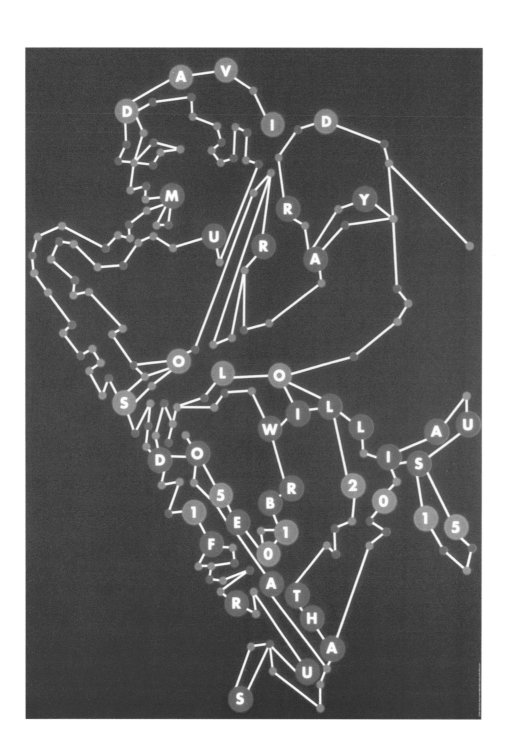

CA
ELECTRONIC

CL
HOMEPRODUCTIONS

DS
ID&D GBR

DE
NATSUMI KOMATSU
BERLIN GERMANY

TY
BANK GOTHIC
LETTER GOTHIC

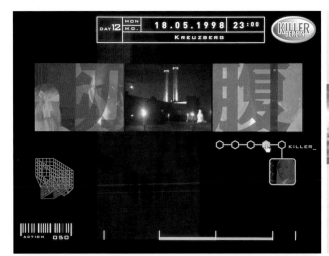

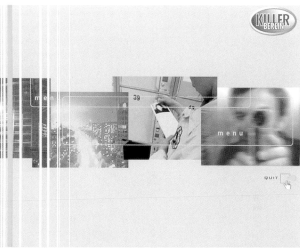

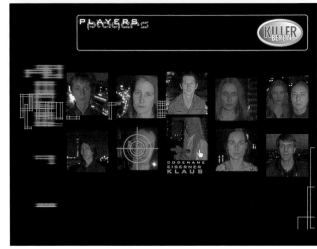

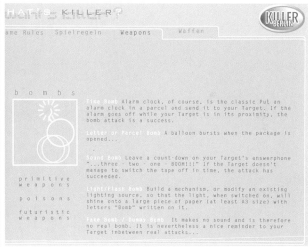

162
ANNUAL REPORT

CA
ANNUAL REPORT

DS
PENTAGRAM

CL
ZURICH CAPITAL MARKETS

DE
SU MATHEWS
HSIN-YING WU
NEW YORK NY

AD
MICHAEL GERICKE
SU MATHEWS

IL
CHRISTIAN NORTHEAST

TY
TRADE GOTHIC
TSABON-4042

DM
11.25 X 7.5 IN
28.6 X 19.1 CM

SUCCESS BEGINS WITH EXPERIENCE AND AN OPEN MIND

X/E IS THE FOUNDAT OF SUCCESSFUL IN ING.

X/E IS ENOUGH. 4 ZCM. WHILE

AL KNOW T IT IS AN ADEQUATE MAP

UNDER ING HOW NEW E OMIC 4 CES R

NAMICS- , MORE IMP T LY, 2 RECOGN

CREATED-IN ORS D A NEW PECTIVE A

RISK MAXIM RET . ZCM UNDER S

USUALLY FOUND W NO 1 ELSE HAS EXPLORED

B 2 EVERY CL ENGAGEMENT: R EMPHASIS ON

X PER TT, OUR ATTITUDE, R AGILITY

BY BINING THESE AT UTES BETTER

OP A TOM D ST EGY A SET OF

-FROM S TURED FIN INGS FUND

MORE. UNDER ING IN :

EVERY 1 🐽 THAT, 👉 4 SOME IN🏇ORS,

RECOGN👀 T🎩 THE PAST 🥫 OFFER VALUABLE GUI🕺

4 TODAY'S FAST 🌰ING IN🏇ING LANDS 🎩

ALTER💍 👉 REDE🦈ING 21ST ①¢RE MARKET

THE NEW IN🏇MENT 🍎FALLS 👉 OPPOR🎵ATT🐝ING

WILLINGNESS 2 TR👁Y INNOVATIVE METH👤 2 MANAGE

😮oui KNOW T🎩 THE GR8TEST REWARDS R

IT IS AN ATTITUDE T🎩 INFORMS THE 5 🗝🎩👔UTES 😮oui

COLLABORATIVE THOUGHT, R RISK 🧔AGEMENT

IN THE MARKET, 👉 R VAST PRO🐟 RESOURCES.

UNDER🧎 THE UNIQUE NEEDS OF EACH ZCM CL👁🐜

RISK-🧔AGED INST🍾🐜 2 💧L I👟 AT

V🐷LL 2 🦌RIVATIVES 👉 🕯🕯 1+1VANTAGED DEBT

IT IS A POWERFUL 🪮🗑A🐦 THAT SETS ZCM A👥.

CA
ANNUAL REPORT

CL
ASPECT COMMUNICATIONS

DS
CAHAN & ASSOCIATES

DE
BOB DINETZ
SAN FRANCISCO CA

AD
BILL CAHAN
BOB DINETZ

CD
BILL CAHAN

PH
TARYN SIMON
MARK LYON
JASON NOCITO
TONY ARRUZA
PAUL JASMIN
GRAHAM MACINDOE

TY
KAATSKILL

DM
8.1 X 10.5 IN
20.6 X 26.7 CM

ASPECT
Communications
2000
Annual
Report

But
it's not the
PRICE
of the flight,
the
COVER
of the book,
or the
COLOR
of
the bedspread.

Whether
rescheduling
a trip,
purchasing
a novel,
or
confirming
a hotel reservation,
customers expect
COORDINATION
among
company divisions
and
contact points and
believe that
SERVICE
is the key
DIFFERENTIATOR
for winning
and
keeping
their business.

ASPECT
enables
companies to
RECOGNIZE
their customers
and
treat each one
INDIVIDUALLY.

THERE

IS

A

DIFFERENCE

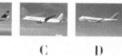

A   B   C   D   E

Five flights from New York to Paris.

1   2   3   4

Four science fiction books.

I   II   III   IV   V   VI

Six hotel rooms in Palm Springs.

CA
POSTER

DS
ZUAN CLUB

CL
D CREATIVE INC.

DE
AKIHIKO TSUKAMOTO
TOKYO JAPAN

AD
AKIHIKO TSUKAMOTO

PT
TWIN-EIGHT CO., LTD.

TY
GILL SANS EXTRA BOLD

DM
40.6 X 28.7 IN
103 X 72.8 CM

CA
POSTER

CL
DAY BY DAY

DS
TERAHIMA DESIGN CO.

DE
MASAYUKI TERASHIMA
SAPPORO JAPAN

AD
MASAYUKI TERASHIMA

TY
HANDMADE

DM
40.6 X 28.7 IN
103 X 72.8 CM

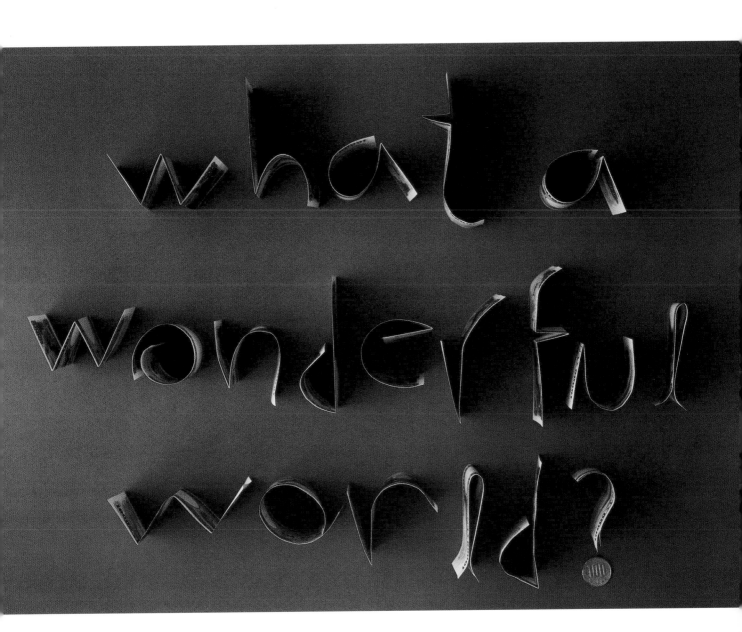

CA
BOOK

AG
GROOTHUIS, LOHFERT,
CONSORTEN

CL
OFFIZIN BERTELSMANN
DER CLUB

DE
RAINER GROOTHUIS
HAMBURG GERMANY

AD
RAINER GROOTHUIS

CD
RAINER GROOTHUIS

PD
ANTJE PRATESI
HAMBURG GERMANY
JAN ENNS
WENTORF GERMANY

TY
WALBAUM STANDARD

DM
6 X 9.5 IN
15.3 X 24.2 CM

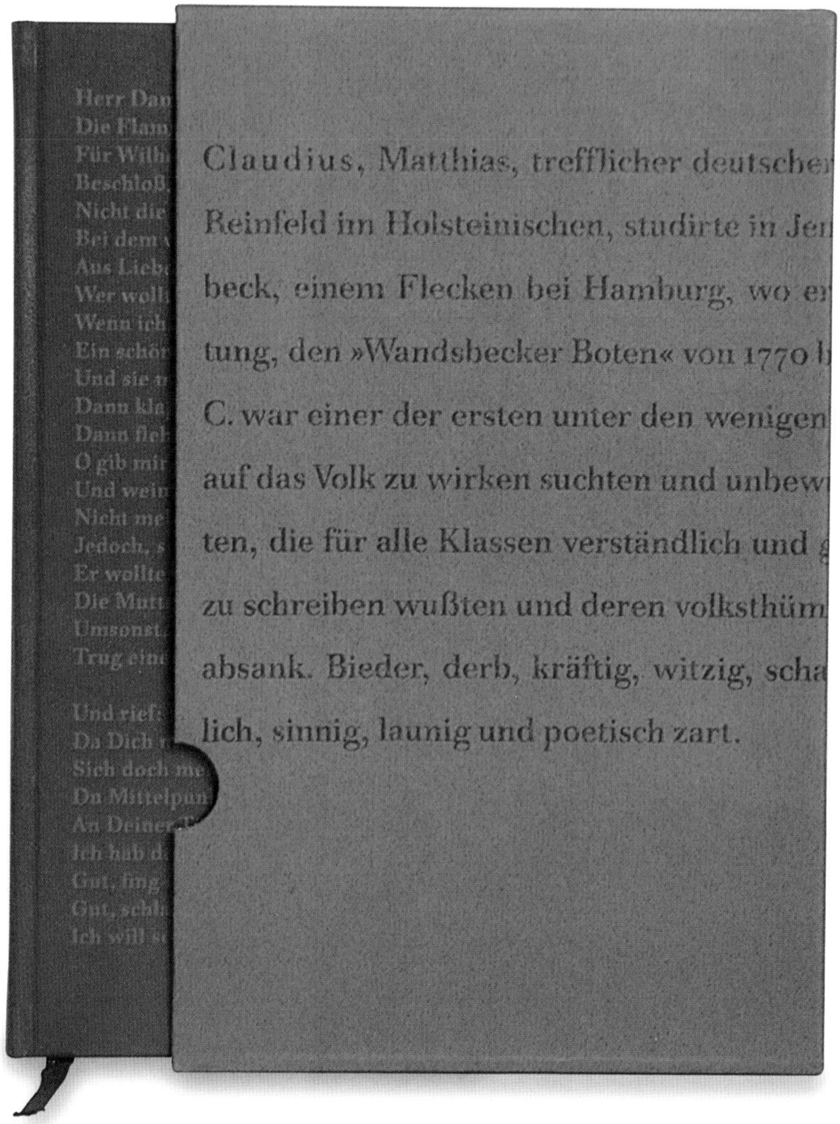

CA
CORPORATE IDENTITY

DS
SHINMURA DESIGN OFFICE

DE
NORITO SHINMURA
TOKYO JAPAN

AD
NORITO SHINMURA

PH
KOGO INOUE

TY
ITC OFFICINA SANS BOLD

DM
VARIOUS

Norito Shinmura

新村則人

株式会社 新村デザイン事務所
104-0061
東京都中央区銀座6-7-8
精美堂ビル4F
Telephone 03-3572-5042
Facsimile 03-3572-5045

Shinmura Design Office
SeibidoBldg.4F,6-7-8,
Ginza,Tokyo
104-0061 Japan
shinmura@kk.iij4u.or.jp

CA
WEB SITE

DS
LUX DESIGN

DE
KRIS PARK
EFRAT RAFAELI
SAN FRANCISCO CA

AD
LAURA CARY

CD
LAURA CARY

IL
EFRAT RAFAELI

TY
CLARENDON

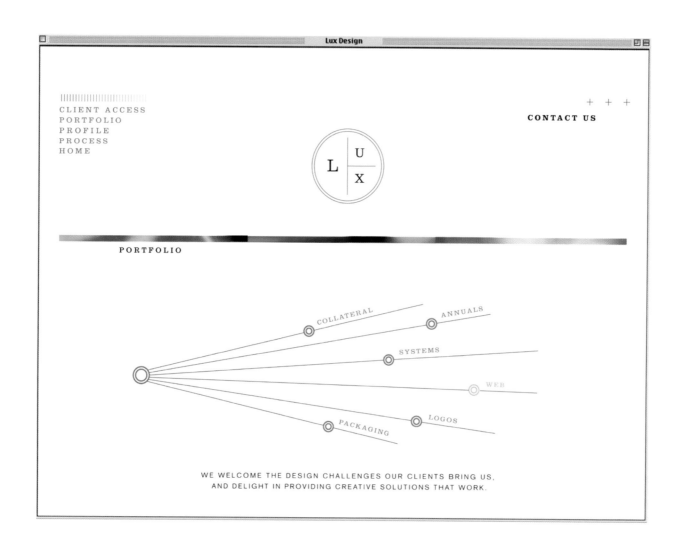

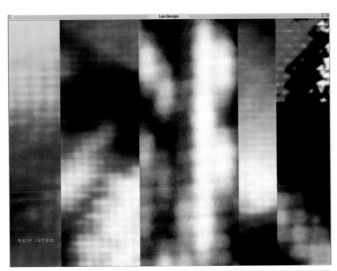

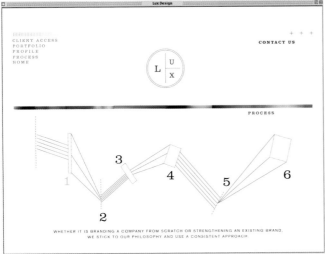

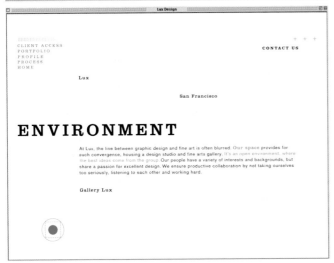

CA
POSTER

CL
W-CLOCK

DS
CID LAB, INC.

DE
YUKICHI TAKADA
OSAKA JAPAN

AD
YUKICHI TAKADA

TY
FRUTIGER BOLD

DM
33.1 X 23.4 IN
84.1 X 59.4 CM

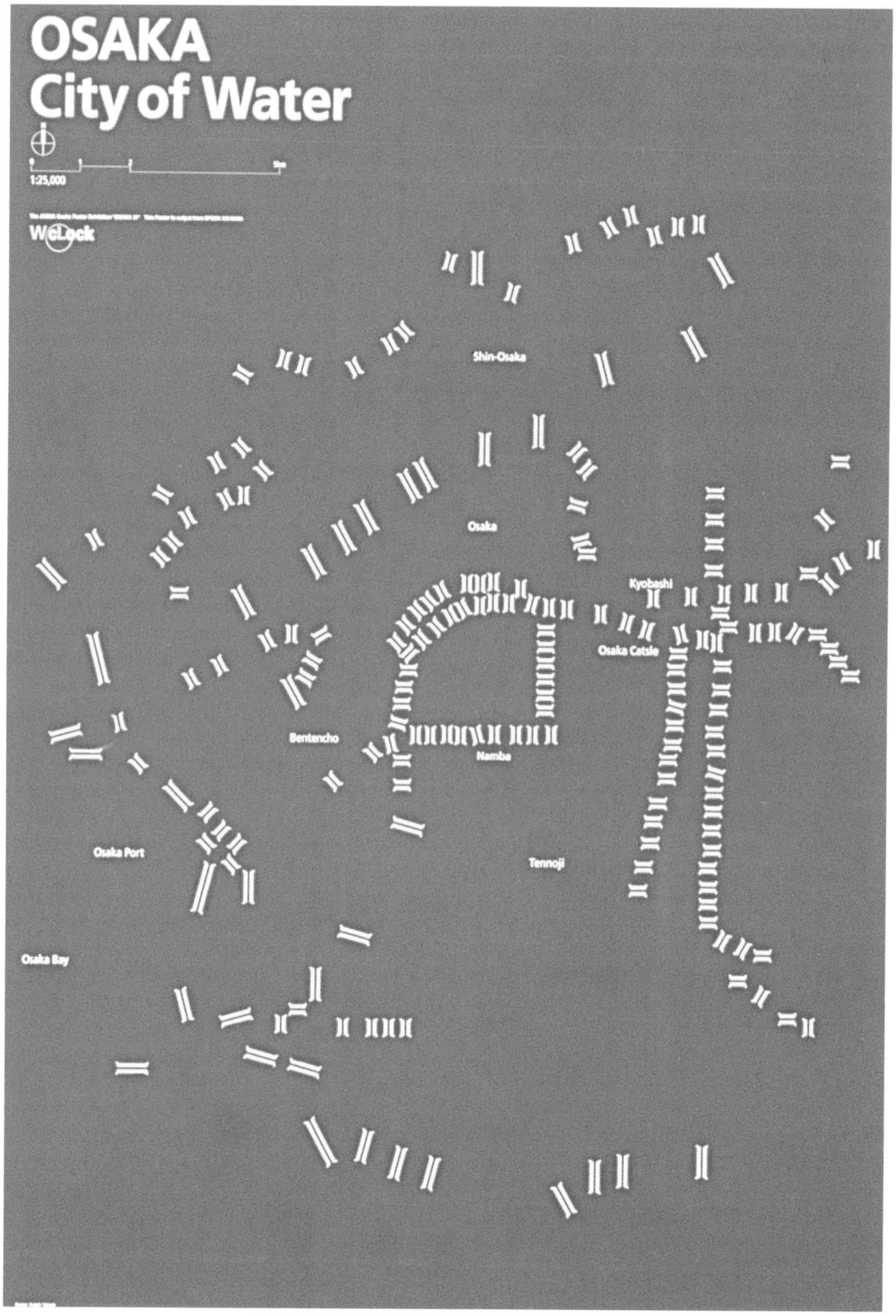

CA
BOOK COVER

CL
UNIVERSITY OF ILLINOIS
PRESS

DE
JILL SHIMABUKURO
CHICAGO IL

AD
COPENHAVER CUMPSTON
CHAMPAIGN IL

TY
DROPLET
META

DM
21 X 9.25 IN
53.3 X 23.5 CM

A NOVEL BY **KAY BOYLE**

p r o c e s s

EDITED AND WITH AN
INTRODUCTION BY SANDRA SPANIER

174

CA
WEB SITE

CL
POTLATCH PAPER

DE
BRIAN JACOBS
HOLGER STRUPPEK
DOUGLAS MCDONALD
BRIAN COX
SAN FRANCISCO CA

DS
PENTAGRAM

AD
KIT HINRICHS

CD
KIT HINRICHS

PH
TERRY HEFFERNAN

CW
DELPHINE HIRASUNE

TY
NEWS GOTHIC

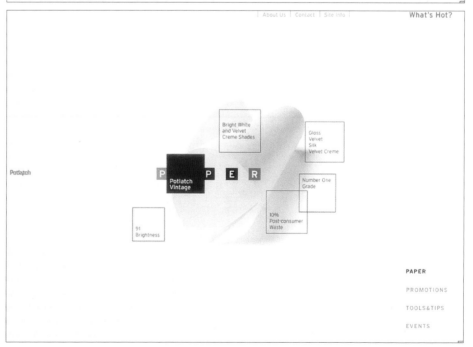

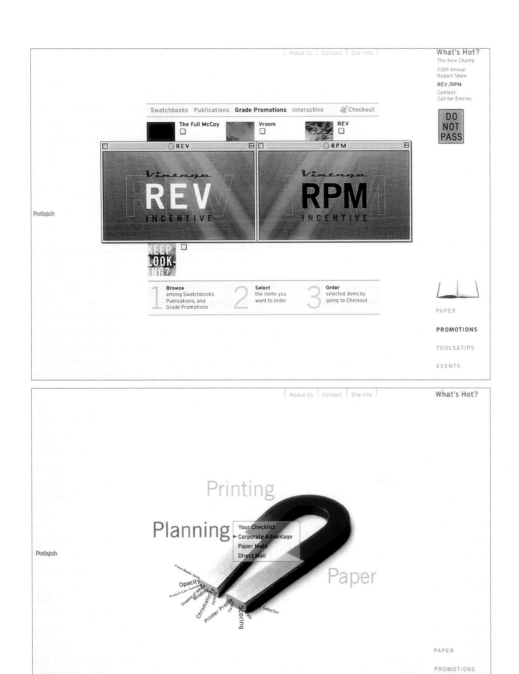

CA
POSTCARDS

DS
TEMPLIN BRINK DESIGN

DE
JOEL TEMPLIN
KRIS DELANEY
SAN FRANCISCO CA

AD
JOEL TEMPLIN
GABY BRINK

CD
JOEL TEMPLIN
GABY BRINK

TY
TRADE GOTHIC

DM
9.5 X 5.5 IN
24.1 X 14 CM

177

CA
TELEVISION COMMERCIAL

AG
GREY WORLDWIDE

DS
BLIND

CL
HASBRO

DE
TOM KOH
STEVE PACHECO
BUCKY FUKUMOTO
SANTA MONICA CA

AD
TOM KOH

CD
CHRIS DO
VANESSA MARZAROLI

IL
BUCKY FUKUMOTO
TOM KOH
VANESSA MARZAROLI
CARLOS RAMOS

AM
EHREN ADDIS
STEVE KASUMA
TOM KOH
PAUL SEYMOUR

FL
THAI KONG

PH
RICK SPITZRASS

ED
ERIK BUTH

EP
ELIZABETH HUMMER

PD
SUSAN APPLEGATE

TY
FRANKFURTER

CA
LOGOTYPE

DS
CHARLES S. ANDERSON
DESIGN

CL
SWIMMING ELEPHANT
PRODUCTIONS

DE
CHARLES S. ANDERSON
TODD PIPER-HAUSWIRTH
ERIK JOHNSON
MINNEAPOLIS MN

AD
CHARLES S. ANDERSON
TODD PIPER-HAUSWIRTH

TY
GARAMOND
CUSTOM
VARIOUS

SWIMMING   ELEPHANT

MUSIC   MEDIA

PRODUCTIONS

CA
ANNUAL REPORT

CL
COST PLUS WORLD MARKET

DS
TURNER & ASSOCIATES

DE
JEAN ORLEBEKE
LAURA MILTON
SAN FRANCISCO CA

AD
PHIL HAMLETT

TY
FUTURA

DM
4.9 X 6.6 IN
12.4 X 16.8 CM

CA
ANNUAL REPORT

DS
LEONHARDT:FITCH

CL
THE FREMONT GROUP

DE
STEVE WATSON
LESLEY FELDMAN
SEATTLE WA

AD
STEVE WATSON
LESLEY FELDMAN

IL
STEVE WATSON
LESLEY FELDMAN

TY
BAUER BODONI
FUTURA

DM
7.5 X 11.75 IN
19.1 X 29.8 CM

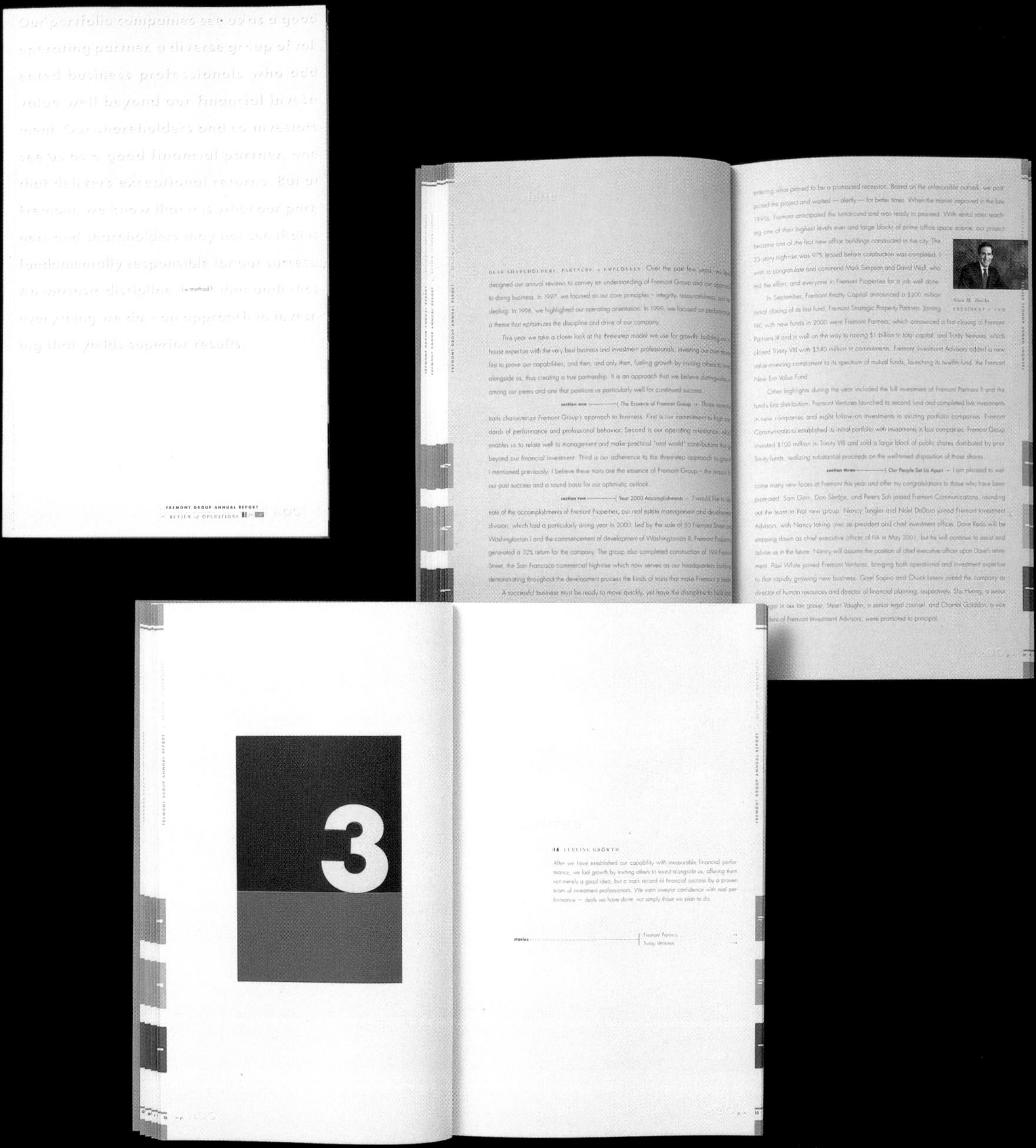

CA
MAGAZINE

DS
LIPPA PEARCE DESIGN

CL
THE TYPOGRAPHIC CIRCLE

DE
DOMENIC LIPPA
MUKESH PARMAR
TWICKENHAM ENGLAND

AD
DOMENIC LIPPA

CB
PATRICK BAGLEE
TOM HINGSTON
DOMENIC LIPPA
RICHARD MCGILLAN

TY
SHAKER
GOTHIC NO. 13

DM
9.25 X 11.2 IN
23.5 X 28.5 CM

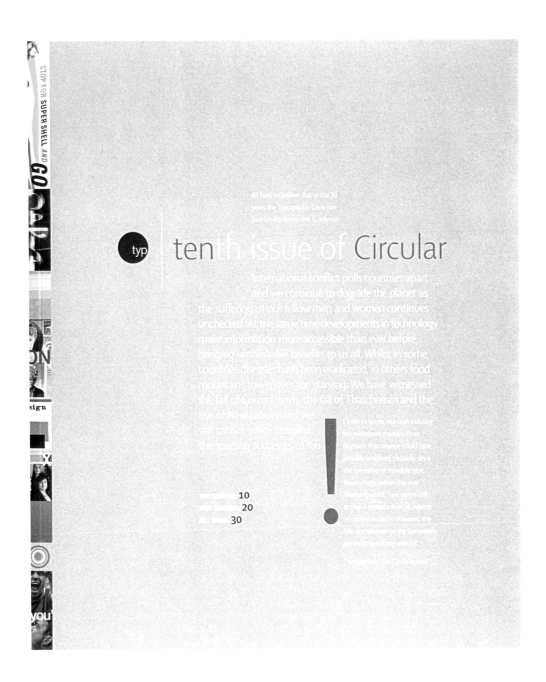

CA
MAGAZINE

DS
HDR VISUAL
COMMUNICATION

CL
BRADBOURNE
PUBLISHING LTD.

DE
HANS DIETER REICHERT
PAUL SPENCER
PAUL ARNOT
PETER BLACK
EAST MALLING ENGLAND

TY
VARIOUS

DM
13.6 X 9.6 IN
34.6 X 24.5 CM

CA
NEWSPAPER

CL
SCHAUSPIELFRANKFURT

DS
P. AGENTUR FÜR
MARKENGESTALTUNG GMBH

DE
TANJA PORALLA
SVEN RITTERHOFF
HAMBURG GERMANY

CD
LO BREIER

PH
DANIEL ANGERMAYR
HENRIK SPOHLER
FRANK RÖTH

TY
AKZIDENZ GROTESK

DM
15.9 X 22.8 IN
40.5 X 58 CM

// Gold
92 bars in a
crashed car

CA
BOOK

CL
ROTTERDAM MUNICIPAL
PORT MANAGEMENT

DS
PROFORMA, STRATEGY,
DESIGN, AND MANAGEMENT

DE
ERNIE ENKELAAR
PAUL SCHOLTE
ROTTERDAM
THE NETHERLANDS

AD
JOOP RIDDER

CD
JOOP RIDDER

ED
ROB WILKEN

CM
COR DE KONING

TY
GOTHIC
NOBEL

DM
11.5 X 13.6 IN
29.5 X 34.5 CM

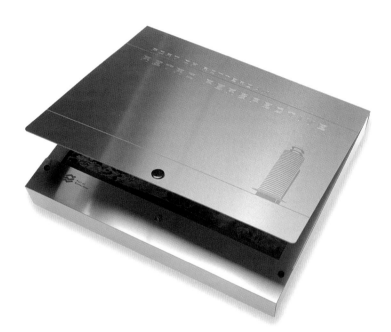

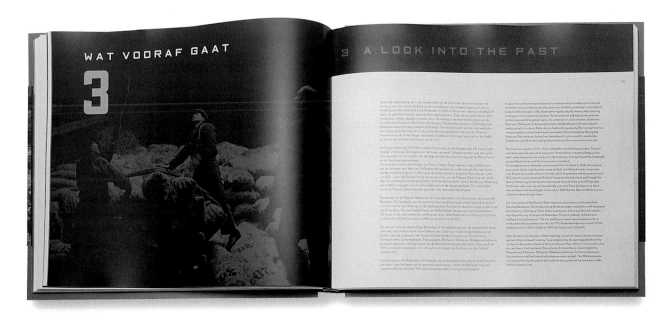

CA
PACKAGING

DS
DOYLE PARTNERS

CL
VIRGIN RECORDS AMERICA
LUAKA BOP

DE
JOHN CLIFFORD
ARIEL APTE
NEW YORK NY

CD
STEPHEN DOYLE

PH
STEPHEN DOYLE

TY
AKZIDENZ GROTESK

DM
5.5 X 5 IN
14 X 12.7 CM

CA
BOOK COVER

DS
FLAME, INC.

CL
JAPAN INDUSTRIAL DESIGN
PROMOTION ORGANIZATION

DE
MASAYOSHI KODAIRA
TOKYO JAPAN

AD
MASAYOSHI KODAIRA

PH
KOZO TAKAYAMA

TY
DIN

DM
8.3 X 11.7 IN
21 X 29.7 CM

CA
BROCHURE

DS
BC DESIGN

DE
DAVID BATES
MIKE CALKINS
SEATTLE WA

AD
DAVID BATES
MIKE CALKINS

TY
HELVETICA

DM
17 X 23 IN
43.2 X 58.4 CM

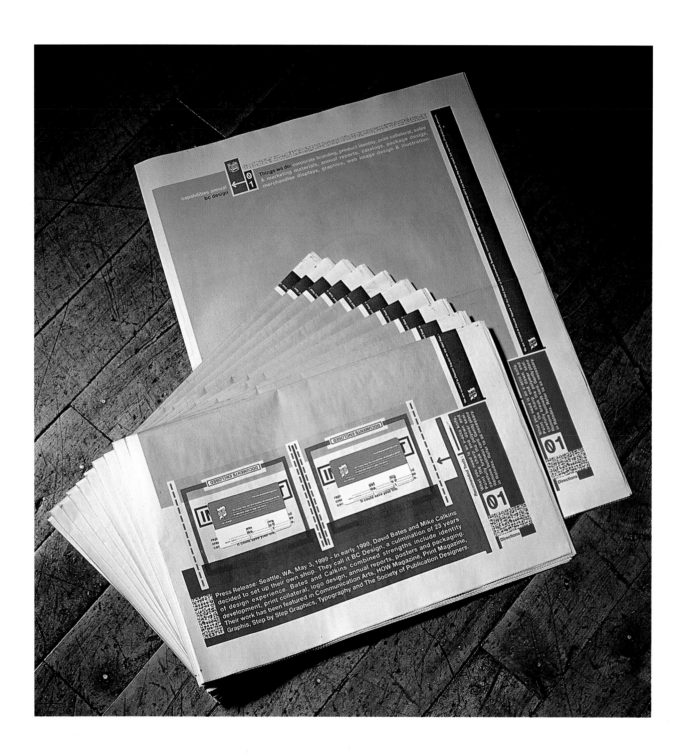

CA
BOOK

DS
MUTABOR DESIGN

AD
CARSTEN RAFFEL
HAMBURG GERMANY

CD
JOHANNES PLASS

PB
GESTALTEN VERLAG BERLIN

TY
MRS. EAVES
TRADE GOTHIC EXTENDED

DM
8.1 X 5.7 IN
20.5 X 14.5 CM

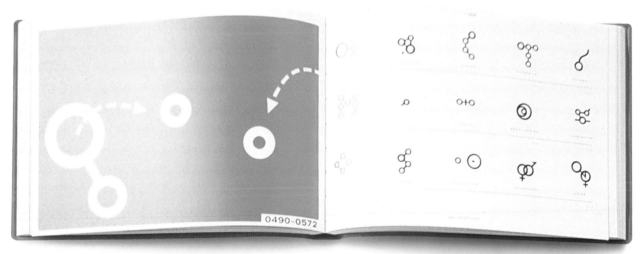

CA
BOOK

DS
BOTSCHAFT GERTRUD NOLTE
VISUELLE KOMMUNIKATION
UND GESTALTUNG

CL
PROF. DR. BAZON BROCK
DUMONT BUCHVERLAG

DE
GERTRUD NOLTE
DÜSSELDORF GERMANY

AD
GERTRUD NOLTE

CD
GERTRUD NOLTE

TY
DIN MITTELSCHRIFT
FRANKLIN GOTHIC
SCALA SERIF

DM
8.3 X 11.7 IN
21 X 29.7 CM

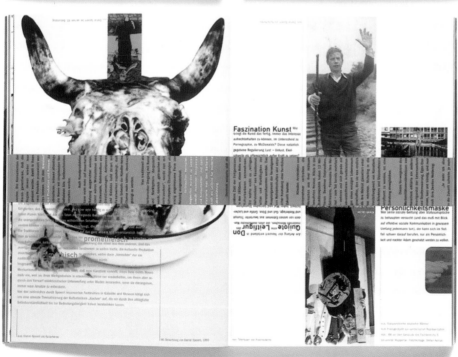

CA
BOOK

DS
KOCHAN & PARTNER

CL
PROKON VERLAG

DE
RON IMELAUER
BORIS KOCHAN
ULRICH MÜLLER
GABRIELE WERNER
MUNICH GERMANY

AD
RON IMELAUER
BORIS KOCHAN
ULRICH MÜLLER
GABRIELE WERNER

CD
RON IMELAUER
BORIS KOCHAN
ULRICH MÜLLER
GABRIELE WERNER

PH
HARALD FREY

TY
GARAMOND
NEWS GOTHIC

DM
7.25 X 5 IN
18.5 X 12.5 CM

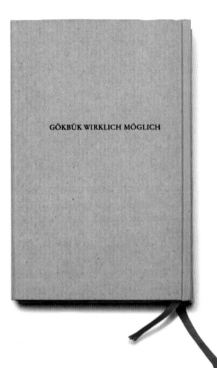

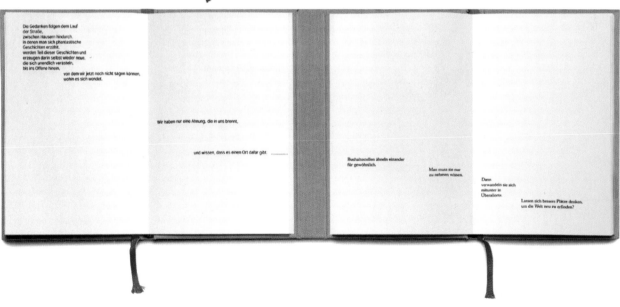

CA
SELF-PROMOTION

DS
THE VALENTINE GROUP

DE
ROBERT VALENTINE
DAVID MEREDITH
NEW YORK NY

CD
ROBERT VALENTINE

IL
BRIAN MCDONOUGH
SALT LAKE CITY UT

TY
HOEFLER TEXT

DM
VARIOUS

CA
CORPORATE IDENTITY

DS
THE VALENTINE GROUP

DE
ROBERT VALENTINE
DAVID MEREDITH
NEW YORK NY

CD
ROBERT VALENTINE

TY
HOEFLER TEXT

DM
7.25 X 10.5 IN
18.4 X 26.7 CM

CA
CATALOG

CL
MINNEAPOLIS COLLEGE OF
ART AND DESIGN

DS
STUDIO D DESIGN

DE
LAURIE DEMARTINO
MINNEAPOLIS MN

AD
LAURIE DEMARTINO

CW
ANASTASIA FAUNCE

PH
GENE PITTMAN
RIK SFERRA
DEAN WILSON

TY
NEWS GOTHIC

DM
5.25 X 8 IN
13.3 X 20.3 CM

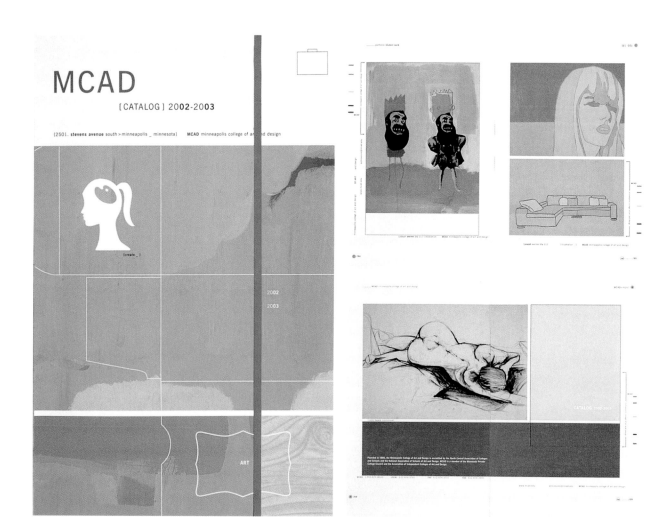

197

[greta weber.senior]

life>passion>art

Throughout its history, MCAD has been characterized by innovation and experimentation. Today, in the twenty-first century, the College continues its tradition of embracing new disciplines and teaching methods, and is committed to self-evaluation and maintaining its place as one of the finest art education facilities in the country.

MCAD

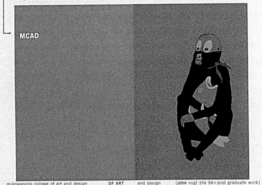

minneapolis college of art and design   OF ART   and design   [john vogt.bfa 98>post graduate work]

One of the most important things that MCAD did for me was to validate that being an artist is serious business—it takes so much work to successfully transform ideas and thoughts into something visually compelling and intellectually rich. This is the kind of environment that fosters emerging artists and it's invaluable to have people around you who are working through successes and failures and who realize the immense amount of time and work that goes into the creative process.
Corinne Wright, BFA '01, South Portland, Maine

MCAD minneapolis college of art and design

www.mcad.edu   admissions@mcad.edu   MCAD minneapolis college of art and design

CA
BROCHURE

DS
LAMBERT UND LAMBERT

DE
MIRIAM LAMBERT
NINA LAMBERT
DÜSSELDORF GERMANY

AD
MIRIAM LAMBERT
NINA LAMBERT

TY
DIN
REGULAR ALTERNATE

DM
6 X 8.5 IN.
15 X 21.5 CM

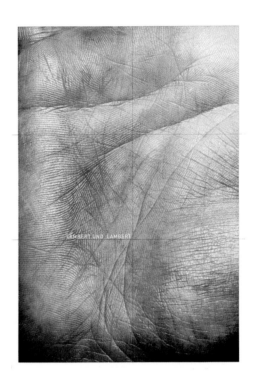

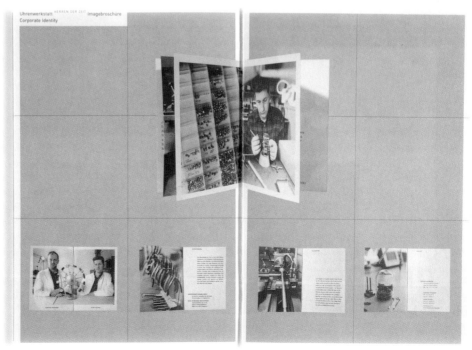

projekt und kommunikation HORIZONT8 Corporate Identity

Design und Distributions e15 Kataloggestaltung
Corporate Identity | Messeeinladung

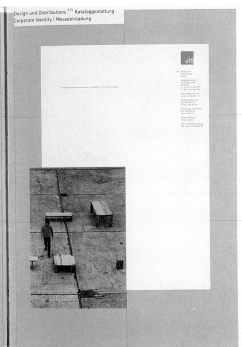

WIR SCHLIESSEN BÜCHER ZUERST INS HERZ UND DANN IN DEN SCHRANK.

Buchgestaltung liegt uns besonders am Herzen: Texte lesen, Bilder sichten, alles sammeln,
anordnen und mit Post-it spicken, auswählen, vergleichen und das meiste davon wieder verwerfen,
um dann noch mal von vorn anzufangen, Konzept aufsetzen, konsequent einer Form folgen und
sich in vielen Schritten dem Punkt nähern, wo man mit wenigen Elementen auskommt, die variabel
sind, immer wieder neu überraschen und sich schon mitteilen, bevor wir sie verstehen.

CA
ADVERTISEMENT

AG
HAKUHODO INC.

DS
JJD
NAKAJO OFFICE
ANDESS INC.
SAITO DESIGN OFFICE

CL
THE YASUDA FIRE & MARINE
INSURANCE CO., LTD.

DE
SHIGEYUKI TAKAOKA
MAIKA SAITO
TOKYO JAPAN

AD
SHIGEYUKI TAKAOKA

CD
RYUICHIRO HARA

LT
MASAYOSHI NAKAJO

FD
ICHIRO TANIDA

TY
ORIGINAL TYPE

CA
INVITATION

DS
JOHNSTON DUFFY

DE
CHRISTINE JOHNSTON
MARTIN DUFFY
PHILADELPHIA PA

AD
CHRISTINE JOHNSTON
MARTIN DUFFY

TY
BAKER SCRIPT
DIN NEUZEIT
VARIOUS ANTIQUE
TYPEFACES

DM
4.25 X 6.25 IN
10.8 X 15.9 CM

CA
BOOK

CL
KATE SPADE

DS
MICHAEL IAN KAYE

DE
MICHAEL IAN KAYE
NEW YORK NY

AD
MICHAEL IAN KAYE

CD
KATE SPADE
ANDY SPADE

TY
ITC NEW BASKERVILLE

DM
9.5 X 9.5 IN
24.1 X 24.1 CM

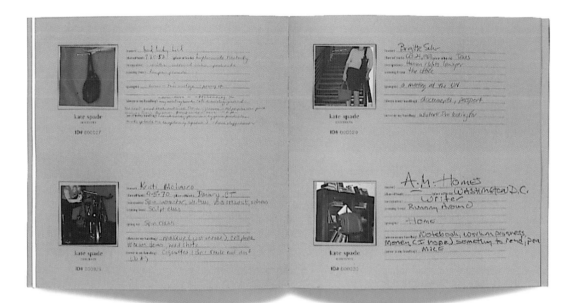

CA
PACKAGING

DS
BC DESIGN

CL
PYRAMID BREWERIES

DE
MIKE CALKINS
DAVID BATES
SEATTLE WA

AD
MIKE CALKINS
DAVID BATES

TY
GLOUCESTER
FRANKLIN GOTHIC
SMOKLER BOLD TITLE
HANDLETTERING

DM
VARIOUS

CA
BOOK

DS
REMPEN & PARTNER:
DAS DESIGN BÜRO

AD
MARGARETE JARZOMBEK
MARK ULRICH
DÜSSELDORF GERMANY

CD
STEFAN BAGGEN

CY
MARGARETE JARZOMBEK
MARK ULRICH

TY
FUTURA
NINETYFIVE

DM
6.3 X 7.25 IN
16 X 18.5 CM

CA
STUDENT PROJECT

SC
SCHOOL OF VISUAL ARTS

DE
CHAD ROBERTS
NEW YORK NY

IN
LOUISE FILI
TRACY BOYCHUK
JEN RODDIE

TY
HELVETICA
TARZANA

DM
5 X 4 IN
12.7 X 10.2 CM

CA
STUDENT PROJECT

SC
ART CENTER COLLEGE
OF DESIGN

DE
SIMON GRENDENE
PASADENA CA

IN
DANIELLE FOUSHEE

TY
CUSTOM FONT
VARIOUS

DM
8 X 9.5 IN.
20.3 X 24.1 CM

CA
STUDENT PROJECT

DS
SCHOOL OF VISUAL ARTS

DE
LAUREN PANEPINTO
NEW YORK NY

IN
GENEVIEVE WILLIAMS
JAMES VICTORE

TY
TIMES NEW ROMAN

DM
5.25 X 5 IN
13.3 X 12.7 CM

Education of the Client
     Occasionally a client will feel that a design
direction is rash, impossible, or simply "not them". This
client will require education by the designer until the client
sees the benefits of trusting the designer.

fig 13.1 Education of the Client

208

CA
STUDENT PROJECT

SH
STATE ACADEMY OF ART
AND DESIGN STUTTGART

AG
STAPELBERG UND FRITZ

DE
MAIK STAPELBERG
DANIEL FRITZ
STUTTGART GERMANY

AD
MAIK STAPELBERG
DANIEL FRITZ

CD
MAIK STAPELBERG
DANIEL FRITZ

LT
WWW.SINUTYPE.COM

TY
AKZIDENZ GROTESK
ST ASE
ST BILLET
ST INVADER
ST SUN CORPORATE
ST VARIO

DM
12.6 X 9.4 IN
32 X 24 CM

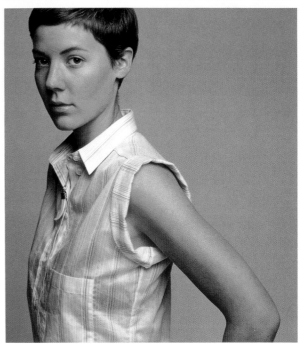

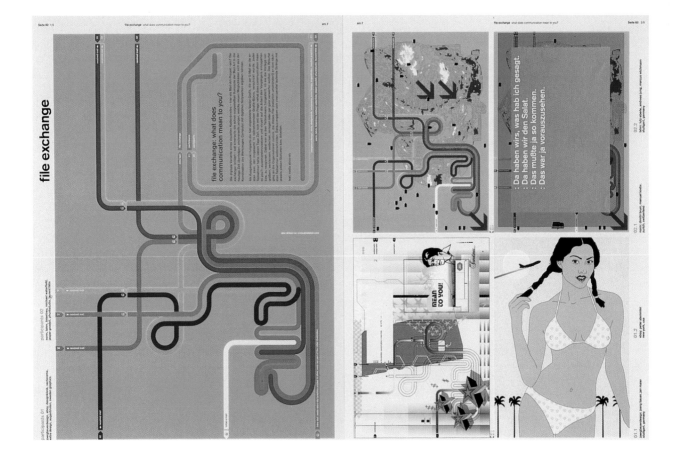

CA
STUDENT PROJECT

SC
SCHOOL OF VISUAL ARTS

DE
SHIGETO AKIYAMA
NEW YORK NY

LT
SHIGETO AKIYAMA

IN
CARIN GOLDBERG

TY
VARIOUS

DM
2 X 7.5 IN
5.1 X 19.1 CM

CA
STUDENT PROJECT

SC
PRATT INSTITUTE

DE
HYUN-JU HWANG
NEW YORK NY

IN
J. OLGA G. DE LA ROZA

TY
FRUTIGER LIGHT

DM
6.5 X 4.5 IN
16.5 X 11.4 CM

Panzotti
Friangoli
Gnocchi
Caramelle

Agnolotti
Fagottini
Tortelloni
Ravioli
Cappelletti

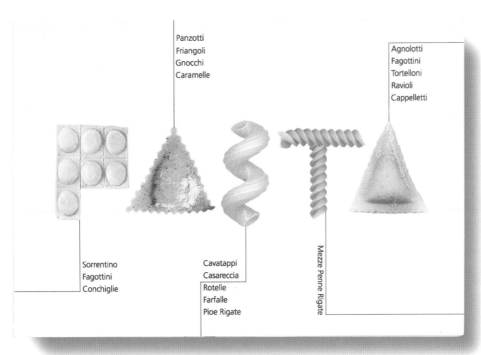

Sorrentino
Fagottini
Conchiglie

Cavatappi
Casareccia
Rotelle
Farfalle
Pioe Rigate

Mezze Penne Rigate

Habanero
Anaheim
Apache
Bird's eye

Italian Sweet, Nu Mex Sunrise, Rococto

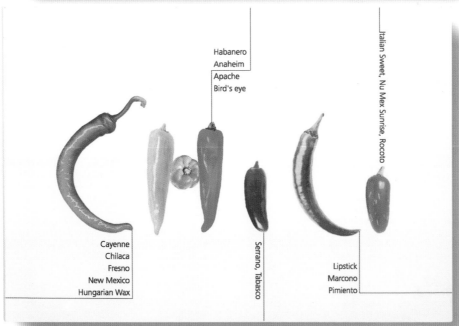

Cayenne
Chilaca
Fresno
New Mexico
Hungarian Wax

Serrano, Tabasco

Lipstick
Marcono
Pimiento

CA
STUDENT PROJECT

SC
PFORZHEIM UNIVERSITY OF
APPLIED SCIENCES

DE
DIRK WACHOWIAK
STUTTGART GERMANY

IN
ULI CLASS
ANDREAS HEMM

TY
GENERATION A
GENERATION AZA
GENERATION AZ
GENERATION ZAZ
GENERATION Z
GENERATION MUTANT
GENERATION SCREEN

DM
10.8 X 6.5 IN
27.5 X 16.5 CM

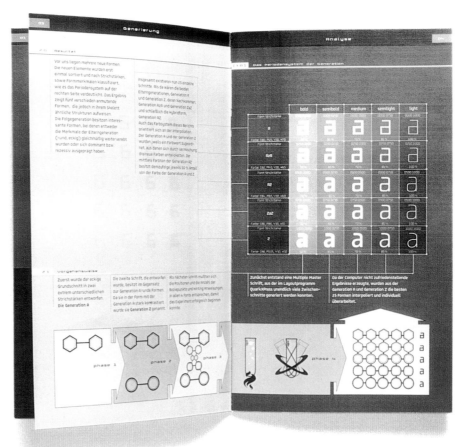

213

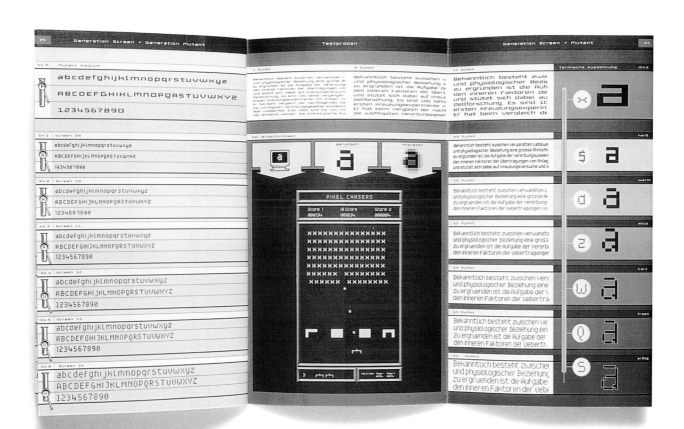

CA
STUDENT PROJECT

SC
SCHOOL OF VISUAL ARTS

DE
SHIGETO AKIYAMA
NEW YORK NY

IN
CARIN GOLDBERG

TY
EMPEROR TEN

DM
VARIOUS

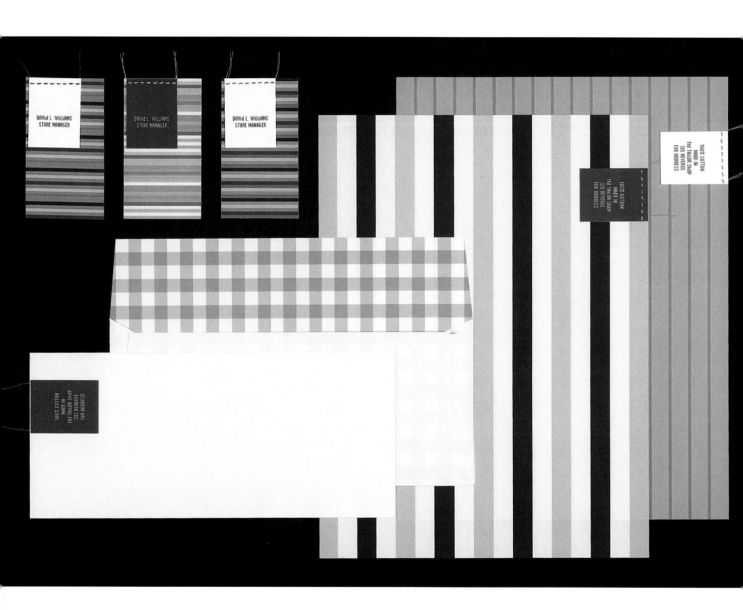

215

CA
STUDENT PROJECT

SC
SCHOOL OF VISUAL ARTS

DE
SHIGETO AKIYAMA
NEW YORK NY

LT
SHIGETO AKIYAMA

IN
CARIN GOLDBERG

TY
ALTERNATE GOTHIC NO. 2

DM
8.5 X 20 IN
21.6 X 50.8 CM

CA
STUDENT PROJECT

SC
UNIVERSITY OF THE ARTS
HDK, BERLIN

DE
FRANZISKA MORLOK
BERLIN GERMANY

IN
HOLGER MATTHIES

TY
THE SANS
EUROSTILE
OCR A
LETTER GOTHIC

DM
VARIOUS

Das Leben ist w ei

Das Leben ist w inStr

Das Leben ist w inSt m

Das Leben ist wie ein Strom, der von seinem Ur

Das Leben ist wie ein Strom, der von seinem

CA
STUDENT PROJECT

DS
SCHOOL OF VISUAL ARTS

DE
JUNE KIM
JERSEY CITY NJ

TY
MYRIAD
CUSTOM

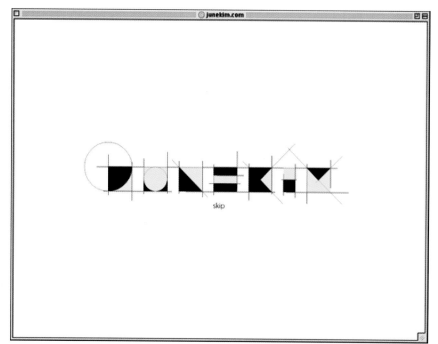

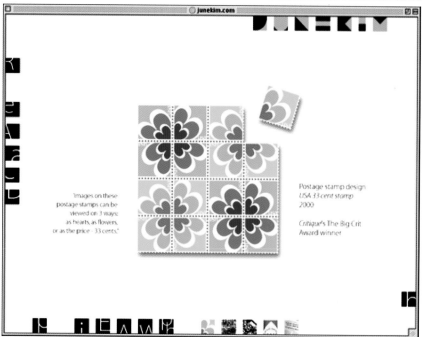

Images on these
postage stamps can be
viewed on 3 ways:
as hearts, as flowers,
or as the price - 33 cents."

Postage stamp design
USA 33 cent stamp
2000

Critique's The Big Crit
Award winner

CA
STUDENT PROJECT

SC
SCHOOL OF VISUAL ARTS

DE
NATASHA D. S. JEN
NEW YORK NY

IN
CARIN GOLDBERG

TY
VARIOUS

DM
VARIOUS

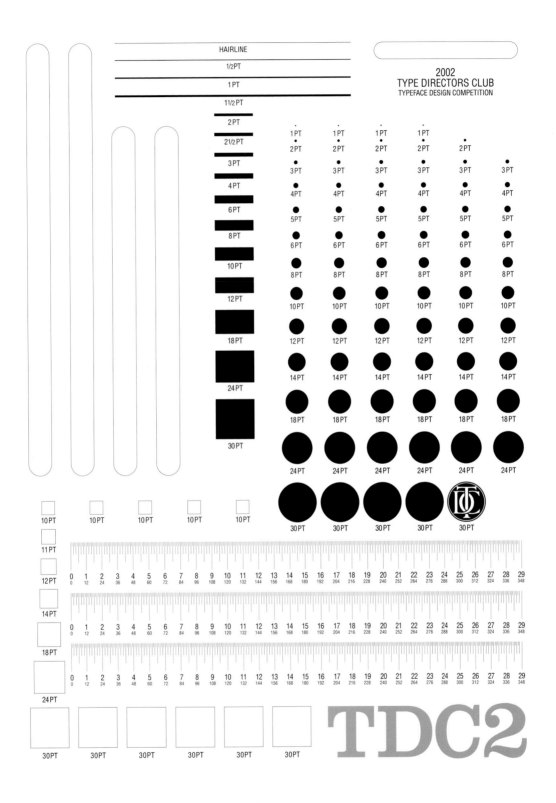

HAIRLINE

1/2 PT

1 PT

1 1/2 PT

2 PT

2 1/2 PT

3 PT

4 PT

6 PT

8 PT

10 PT

12 PT

18 PT

24 PT

30 PT

2002
TYPE DIRECTORS CLUB
TYPEFACE DESIGN COMPETITION

1 PT

2 PT

3 PT

4 PT

5 PT

6 PT

8 PT

10 PT

12 PT

14 PT

18 PT

24 PT

30 PT

10 PT   10 PT   10 PT   10 PT   10 PT

11 PT

12 PT

14 PT

18 PT

24 PT

30 PT   30 PT   30 PT   30 PT   30 PT   30 PT

TDC2

CH
GARY MUNCH

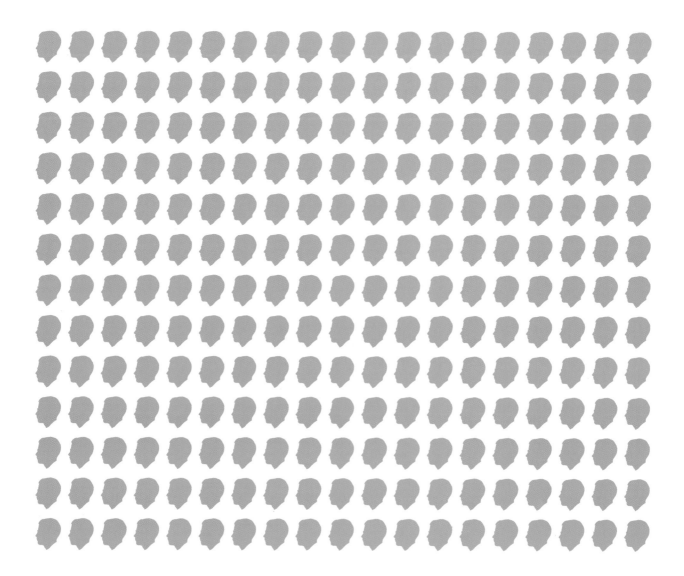

Type design is a peculiar thing, for peculiar people – people who can see the individual twigs on a tree and yet also hold the forest in the same view. Endless details in a thousand permutations must all be combined to make a harmonious whole that retains its integrity no matter the combinations and recombinations the individual parts make.

Such flexibility of use is unusual in most design fields, where the final layout, or design, or construction is fixed in proportion, disposition of shapes, color, and substance. Type designers must instead consider each combination of each of the lettershapes and provide for unique combinations that might occur seldom in one text but frequently in another, in varied sizes and line lengths, and still provide pleasing textures, ease of reading, and lively and meaningful variety of form and expression. The result of this craftsmanship is exhibited in the various designs selected by the jury of the TDC2 2002 type design competition. From the many entries sent from the world over, fifteen were chosen to represent the best in type design for the previous year, 2001.

The winning entries, selected by Jill Bell, John Downer, Dennis Pasternak, and Richard Weltz, range from the reasoned textual calligraphics of Robert Slimbach's Brioso to Jim Parkinson's cheekily cheery Keester; from the clean geometrics of Mutabor Design's Media Core 3 to the compatible widths and styles of Atelier h's Siemens; from the nostalgia of Nick Curtis's Woodley Park to the comicbook favorites of Robin Spehar's Dreamer DD; from the historical revival of Andreu Balius's Pradell to the new historicity of Kent Lew's Whitman. It was a pleasure to see so many well-built typefaces entered into the TDC2 2002 and a great pleasure to see the results of the jury's deliberations over the merits of each.

Gary Munch's type design work leans increasingly toward text faces, though an occasional display face is known to wander his hard drives. His designs include, among others, UrbanScrawl, Nanogram, Linotype Ergo, and Linotype Really.

Munch was educated in Eugene, Oregon, earning a BFA at the University of Oregon. There, he studied graphic design and learned and taught calligraphy in the Oregon manner; most memorably he took typography with Chuck "Lucida" Bigelow in the pre-computer days. Munch received an MS from the University of Bridgeport in art education.

Currently teaching at area colleges in Connecticut, Munch hopes to ensure that at least someone knows how, when, and why to type a real quotation mark.

Munch was the chairman of the TDC2 2002 Type Design Competition and is currently the Web messer for the TDC Web site.

JUDGES

JILL BELL
JOHN DOWNER
DENNIS PASTERNAK
RICHARD N. WELTZ

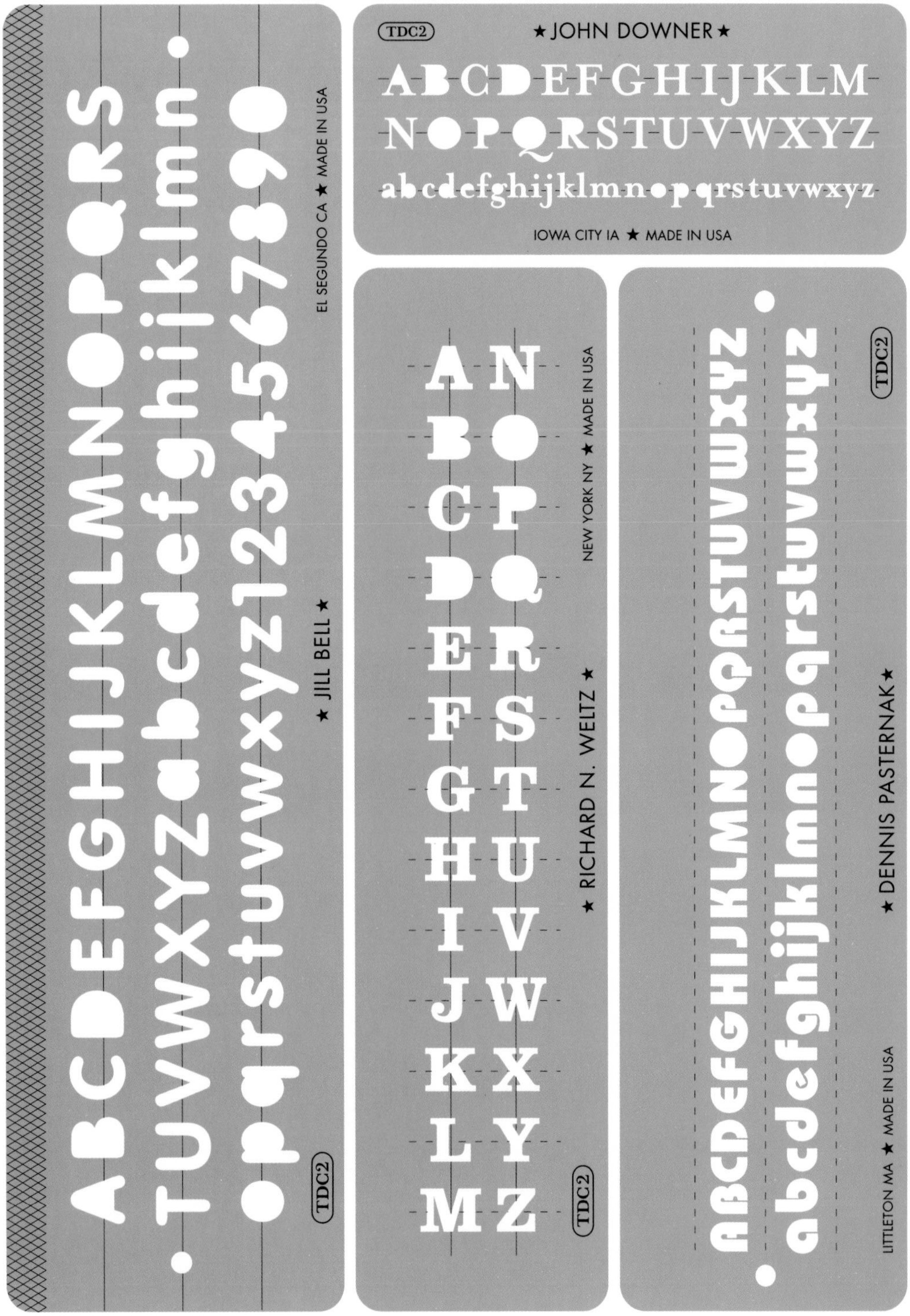

ABCDEFGHIJKLMNOPQRS
TUVWXYZabcdefghijklmn
opqrstuvwxyz1234567890

EL SEGUNDO CA ★ MADE IN USA

★ JILL BELL ★

TDC2

TDC2 ★ JOHN DOWNER ★

ABCDEFGHIJKLM
NOPQRSTUVWXYZ
abcdefghijklmnopqrstuvwxyz

IOWA CITY IA ★ MADE IN USA

A N
B O
C P
D Q
E R
F S
G T
H U
I V
J W
K X
L Y
M Z

NEW YORK NY ★ MADE IN USA

★ RICHARD N. WELTZ ★

TDC2

ABCDEFGHIJKLMNOPQRSTUVWXYZ
abcdefghijklmnopqrstuvwxyz

★ DENNIS PASTERNAK ★

LITTLETON MA ★ MADE IN USA

TDC2

Jill Bell began her career as a lettering artist shortly after an encounter with a Speedball pen in a high school commercial art class. She has worked as a graphic designer primarily doing lettering, calligraphy, and type design for about two decades, with a few respites from the freelance existence: she worked as a signpainter for two years and did a short stint as a production artist for Saul Bass in the 1980s. Bell's typeface designs can be seen in the ITC catalog (Carumba, Clover, Gigi, Hollyweird, and Smack), and in the Agfa-Monotype catalog, which includes her most recent release, Swank. Her face, Bruno, for Adobe reflects an understanding of the written form applied to the regularity of type forms. Her handlettering can be seen online at jillbell.com and in *The Workbook*.

SMACK

GIGI

SWANK

CLOVER

HOLLYWEIRD

John Downer is a sign painter by trade, with a specialty in gold leaf lettering. He has a BFA in fine art from Washington State University and both an MA and an MFA in painting from the University of Iowa. Downer began his career as a freelance type designer in 1983. His many typefaces have been published in the United States by Emigre (Vendetta, Council, and Brothers); by Bitstream (Iowan Oldstyle); by The Font Bureau; and in Milan, Italy, by Design Lab.

Downer writes about type and type history for *Emigre, House,* and other publications. He lives in Iowa City and travels throughout the United States and Europe, always on the lookout for interesting letterforms.

IOWAN OLD STYLE
{1991} published by {2001}
BITSTREAM INC.
Cambridge, Massachusetts

Simona
{with Jane Patterson}
published by
DESIGN LAB
Milan, Italy
1996

PAPERBACK
IN PROGRESS
House Industries
Yorklyn, Delaware

COUNCIL
COUNCIL BLUFFS, IOWA
Published in 1999 by Emigre
SACRAMENTO. CALIFORNIA

VENDETTA
published in 1999 by
EMIGRE
Sacramento, California

Triplex Italic
Published in 1990 by Emigre

IRONMONGER
(PUBLISHED BY THE FONT BUREAU)
1991-1993 BOSTON, MASSACHUSETTS, USA

SamSans
published by
The FONT BUREAU, INC.
Boston, Massachusetts

BROTHERS
published by
EMIGRE
Sacramento. California

With nearly two decades of experience in the study and practice of type design, Dennis Pasternak, is an accomplished designer of original typefaces. Although mathematical curves and patterns populate his computer monitors, Pasternak senses the wood, metal, and brush used by his professional ancestors. Pasternak's body of original designs includes Bitstream Chianti as well as typefaces developed during his tenure at Galápagos Design Group: the Maiandra GD family, Baltra GD, and ITC Stylus. All of Pasternak's designs have traditional roots and are highly readable; they focus on the reader, rather than on their appearance as graphic elements.

Pasternak holds a BFA degree in design from the Massachusetts College of Art. He is a member of the Association Typographique Internationale (ATypl).

Maiandra®

Regular Aa Bb Cc Dd Ee Ff Gg Hh *Italic Ii Jj Kk Ll Mm Nn Oo Pp Qq*

Demibold Rr Ss Tt Uu Vv Ww ***Demibold Italic Xx Yy Zz &1234***

Black Aa Bb Cc Dd Ee Ff Gg ***Black Italic Hh Ii Jj Kk Ll Mm***

JD
RICHARD N. WELTZ

After several years as an advertising agency copywriter and account executive, Richard N. Weltz joined his family's advertising typography firm and has been involved in typeshop management ever since — working his way over some four decades through all the technology changes from hot metal to today's Postscript. He served as president of the Typographers International Association, is the author of dozens of published articles on the typographic business, and has presented seminars to typographic groups in many cities around the country and abroad. Over time, Weltz narrowed his efforts to the field of for-

eign language typography and translation and now heads up the New York City firm, Spectrum Multilanguage Communications. While not laying claim to being a typeface designer by vocation, Weltz designed several Arabic fonts that were licensed and produced by Berthold; a number of others were marketed by VGC as fonts for the PhotoTypositor.

Weltz holds a degree in public and international affairs from the Woodrow Wilson School, Princeton University.

Arabetica

الافكار الى الناس

الافكار الى الناس

Ara-Garde

إن الصحيفة المطبو

Mozaique

الكلمات تنقل الافكار الى

Scarab

إن الصحيفة المطبوعة

Nile

إن الصحيفة المطبوعة

JUDGES' CHOICES

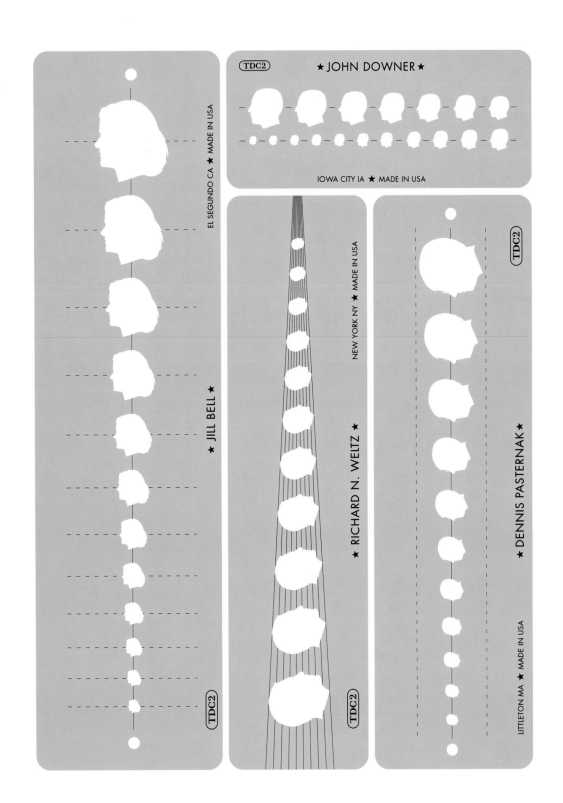

★ JOHN DOWNER ★

TDC2

IOWA CITY IA ★ MADE IN USA

★ JILL BELL ★

EL SEGUNDO CA ★ MADE IN USA

TDC2

★ RICHARD N. WELTZ ★

NEW YORK NY ★ MADE IN USA

TDC2

★ DENNIS PASTERNAK ★

TDC2

LITTLETON MA ★ MADE IN USA

JD
JILL BELL

Evincing a mastery of both type design and traditional handwritten letterforms, Brioso is a lovely, well-produced calligraphic family. I find its classical beauty and proportions immensely attractive, the extensiveness of the family even more alluring. The Brioso family members are an ingenious mix of the best of the Italian Renaissance humanist scripts, adapted to contemporary type and usage. As these calligraphic romans were the model for the earliest Venetian faces (and most subsequent ones as well), their familiarity works well to keep Brioso from being tucked away in too tight a historical or calligraphic niche. And in spite of its pronounced roots, Brioso is also a completely contemporary interpretation of those bookhands and an extremely adept one at that. The characters retain many of the freedoms of a modern, dexterous dance of the pen, particularly visible in the italic swash cap sets. Subtle but pervasive curves throughout the entire family create a lively, spirited quality reflecting handwritten origins.

Designer Robert Slimbach forsakes the more condensed and angular chancery cursive models and proportioned and weighted the italic sets to agree with the romans, creating a harmonious, fluent color. The verity and variety, grace, and utilitarian nature of this family make it suited to a multitude of projects and purposes from text to display. It is beautiful and eminently readable at small sizes. At a grander scale, Brioso fully reveals its sensual, elegant nature.

TD
ROBERT SLIMBACH

Adobe Systems introduces Brioso Pro, a new typeface family designed in the calligraphic tradition of our Latin alphabet. Brioso Pro displays the look of a finely penned roman and italic script, retaining the immediacy of handlettering while having the scope and functionality of a contemporary composition family. Brioso Pro blends the humanity of written forms with the clarity of digital design, allowing designers to set pages of refined elegance.

Designed by Robert Slimbach, this energetic type family is modeled on his formal roman and italic script. In the modern calligrapher's repertoire of lettering styles, roman script is the hand that most closely mirrors the oldstyle types that we commonly use today; it is also among the most challenging styles to master. Named after the Italian word for "lively," words set in Brioso Pro move rhythmically across the page with an energy that is tempered by an ordered structure and lucidity of form.

Brioso Pro is an extended type family consisting of integrated weights, styles, and optical masters.

Its rich character palette is offered in four weights spanning from light to bold and four optical size ranges. The glyph sets include all the characters normally found in expert and standard sets as well as an expanded accented character compliment, additional monetary and math symbols, a collection of alternate characters, swash italic fonts, and a set of ornaments. Brioso Pro also includes a special Light Poster font in roman and italic styles. These fonts are a bit more stylized than the regular designs and are intended for use at very large sizes. The Brioso Pro family of typefaces covers the spectrum of font styles used in modern typography.

As a full-featured OpenType family, Brioso Pro's vast array of glyphs can be activated in page layout programs, either individually, or as style groups, using the fonts feature list. Brioso Pro can be used anywhere the user wants to convey a sense of spontaneity and sophistication. It is ideal for use in personal correspondence, poetry, menus, small press books, letterpress editions, wedding announcements, signage, and display titles.

TF
BRIOSO™ PRO

FD
ADOBE SYSTEMS,
INCORPORATED

TD
ROBERT SLIMBACH
SAN JOSE CA

FA
LIGHT CAPTION
REGULAR CAPTION
SEMIBOLD CAPTION,
BOLD CAPTION
LIGHT TEXT
REGULAR TEXT
SEMIBOLD TEXT
LIGHT SUBHEAD
REGULAR SUBHEAD
SEMIBOLD SUBHEAD
BOLD SUBHEAD
LIGHT DISPLAY
REGULAR DISPLAY
SEMIBOLD DISPLAY
BOLD DISPLAY

Brioso Pro

Brioso Pro is designed in the calligraphic tradition of our Latin alphabet, evoking the look of a finely-penned roman and italic script. Brioso retains the immediacy of hand lettering while having the scope and functionality of a contemporary composition family, blending the organic qualities of written forms with the clarity of digital design.

Adobe designer Robert Slimbach modeled Brioso on his formal roman and italic script. In the modern calligrapher's repertoire of lettering styles, roman script is the hand that most closely mirrors the oldstyle types that we commonly use today, and is among the most challenging styles to master. Brioso moves rhythmically across the page with an energy that is tempered by an ordered structure and lucid form.

Light Caption	Regular Caption	**Semibold Caption**	**Bold Caption**
Light Caption Italic	*Italic Caption*	***Semibold Caption Italic***	***Bold Caption Italic***
Light Text	Regular Text	**Semibold Text**	**Bold Text**
Light Text Italic	*Italic Text*	***Semibold Text Italic***	***Bold Text Italic***
Light Subhead	Regular Subhead	**Semibold Subhead**	**Bold Subhead**
Light Subhead Italic	*Italic Subhead*	***Semibold Subhead Italic***	***Bold Subhead Italic***
Light Display	Regular Display	**Semibold Display**	**Bold Display**
Light Display Italic	*Italic Display*	***Semibold Display Italic***	***Bold Display Italic***
Light Poster			
Light Poster Italic			

These roman and italic text typefaces were, to use the words of their designer, "derived from 18th century Spanish specimens." An accompanying facsimile of those specimens allowed the TDC typeface judges to compare the winning duo with the types that served as the models. Both of the historical types were cut in Madrid by Eudaldo Pradell the elder, sometime before 1780. The sample was printed in 1793. (A reproduction exists in Updike.)

We awarded the honor unanimously. The contestant's expertise in the art of interpretation is apparent. Also in evidence is the art of compromise; for these two digital designs are not, in an absolute sense, outright revivals of Pradell's two types. Instead, there has been a tradeoff between obvious disparities in the original samples and certain hallmarks of the Spanish style. Compare, for example, the way Pradell bracketed the serif of his roman E in the lower-right corner of the letter, but did not follow the same principle in his italic E. In Pradell's era there was no mandate to make the roman and italic capitals as alike one another as possible. Today it is the norm in type families. It's a sign of the times — not necessarily a sign of inattention.

When I study the entry, I see that the designer has a command of drawing and spacing, as well as an ability to use the typefaces advantageously in presentation. The designer's discernment in numerous aspects of type design and typography is admirable. The work is declared a success, because the objective was not only to preserve the historical flavor of the originals, but to make that flavor palatable to our modern tastes. On both counts, this pair of faces wins.

TD
ANDREU BALIUS
PLANELLES

I created Pradell after two years of researching the work of the Catalan punchcutter Eudald Pradell (1721-1788). Although Pradell is completely unknown today — very few specimen books contain his work — he was the most important punchcutter at the end of the 18th century in Spain. He was commissioned by King Carlos III to provide new typefaces for the Imprenta Real in Madrid.

Pradell is a transitional typeface that gently alludes to the modern era of typography. I have incorporated those details that best reflect Eudald Pradell's work, but I have also taken into account those features that make a typeface suitable for reading today. In creating the Pradell family I was inspired by the best in Pradell's work, not by nostalgia. The typeface is my homage to him.

235

TF
PRADELL

FD
ANDREU BALIUS
TYPERWARE

TD
ANDREU BALIUS PLANELLES
BARCELONA SPAIN

FA
ROMAN
ITALIC
BOLD

PRADELL

Pradell Roman, *Italic* & **Bold**.
Latin text family inspired from 18th century spanish type specimens by Andreu Balius

ABC
DEFGHIJK
LMNOPQRSTUVWXYZ

abcdefghijklmnopqrstuvwxyz

(0 1 2 3 4 5 6 7 8 9) • @ © ® ç ń œ å † ‡ : . ;
{ / } " « ø » $ £ ¢ € ct fi fl ß * ? ! § ¶

Eudald Pradell was born in Ripoll *(Catalunya, Spain)*, a little village under the Pyrenees, in 1721. He pertained to a family of gunsmiths and learned the practice of being an armourer with his father, adquiring the knowledge of making punches. ¶ Pradell established his own workshop in Barcelona. Despite he was illiterate, he was able to produce one of the most appreciated typefaces ever cut in Spain. His fame as a punchcutter increased and King Carlos III gave him a pension in order to provide new type designs at the *Imprenta Real* in Madrid, where he finally moved and set up his foundry. He died in 1788 in Barcelona. ¶

Eudald Pradell (1721-1788), was a catalan punchcutter.

HISPANIA
hamburguesa
ROMA
SOUP & NOODLES
Barcelona
What would you like for dinner?
cactus
Typography
Montserrat

The initial overall impression of Whitman was the clarity of the fonts presented. There was a comfortable level of readability with all three individual designs. The italic appeared to be a fine companion to its roman, while not overwhelming or adversely affecting the overall text. The Whitman fonts also appeared to be well-crafted and well-balanced in weight and proportion. I was particularly impressed with the appropriate way the fonts were presented, but found it unfortunate that a bold and bold italic were missing from the family. Those weights would have enhanced the presentation. I also observed that all subgroups within the character set successfully complemented one another and did not call attention to the eye.

At first look the capital set appeared to be inspired by designs such as Jan Van Krimpen's Romulus, Eric Gill's Joanna, and, under Stanley Morison's direction, Monotype's adaption of Simon Fournier's classic design. A closer look revealed a strong influence of Martin Majoor's Scala design. There were subtle differences between Whitman and Scala, such as the serif treatment of the E, F, and T. More noticeable differences can be seen in the S, W, and Y. Similarities between the two designs can be found by comparing the C, G, and O. Without too much more design effort it would be advantageous to the designer to redraw a few of the capitals with more subtle individuality in form, without altering the overall character of the design.

The lowercase in Whitman greatly deviates from the Scala influence in both roman and italic. The roman appears to have subtle influences from Gill's Joanna and W. A. Dwiggins' Caledonia. To design a hybrid from those two designs and do it successfully is a great accomplishment. A hint of Dwiggins can be seen in the counter treatments of the h, m, n, and u. Gill's influence can be seen in the design of the a, c, g, t, w, and y. Overall the lowercase roman sits sturdily on the baseline giving a horizontal appearance to the text and enhancing the ease in reading over an extended period of time. The italic lowercase appears to be a fine complement to the roman. This design also appears to be very successful in its individuality and subtleness, without diminishing the readability of the overall text. The italic angle was very well-thought-out, allowing a speed of reading that matches the roman. The italic design is simply understated with a well-balanced amount of flourish. The oldstyle figures were well-drawn and proportioned, though more thought may have gone into the proportions of the monetary symbols. They could have been proportioned to work better with the ascender height and descender depth of the figures, while complementing the capital and lowercase character sets. It also would have been advantageous to the designer to have a tabular lining figure set since an oldstyle set existed in the small capital font. Two figure sets would enhance the family marketability and increase its range of use in text and display settings.

Overall, despite these qualifications, I feel Whitman could have a long life in usage. It is a very promising text design.

A couple years ago, I acquired an original specimen for Linotype Caledonia — an amazing design in its metal version. I was particularly captivated by Dwiggins's treatment of the counters in the arched letters, h m n u. What if I combined this structure with a contemporary, spartan finish? While the result is unabashedly digital, I tried to infuse Whitman with the traditional values of classic book types. I sought to create a typeface which, although hopefully distinctive, might appear at first glance somewhat ordinary, one which would sit! stay! and behave itself well in text.

Stanley Morison observed that for a good new font to be successful, few should recognize its novelty. Nevertheless, I'm grateful that the TDC2 judges took notice of my design.

TF
WHITMAN

FD
FONT BUREAU

TD
KENT LEW
WASHINGTON MA

FA
ROMAN
SMALL CAPS
ITALIC

Whitman

Roman : SMALL CAPS : *Italic*

TO BE CONCERNED with the shapes of letters is to work in an ancient and fundamental material. The qualities of letter forms at their best are the qualities of a classic time: *order, simplicity, grace.* To try to learn and repeat their excellence is to put oneself under training in a most simple and severe school of design. — W. A. DWIGGINS

ABCDEFGHIJKLMNOPQRSTUVWXYZ

[(ABCDEFGHIJKLMNOPQRSTUVWXYZ&)]

abcdefghijklmnopqrstuvwxyz&fiflffffiffl

$£€#1234567890 ¶ §§$£€#1234567890

ABCDEFGHIJKLMNOPQRSTUVWXYZ

abcdefghijklmnopqrstuvwxyz&fiflffffiffl

[(",.:;?!")] *$£€#1234567890* *[(",.:;?!")]*

JD
RICHARD N. WELTZ

Although many "handwriting" fonts are created, few, if any, especially among those in the genre of connected scripts, demonstrate the charm of the Dearest style. I find it elegant and captivating, and I enjoy the subtle wit of cleverly planned alternate characters, some of which, such as the lowercase f, work attractively both individually and when combined into ligated form. While fully suitable for contemporary use, Dearest beautifully captures the grace of a bygone era.

TD
CHRISTINA TORRE

P22 Dearest was inspired by the script found in a German 19th-century handwritten journal chronicling a history of the Middle Ages. Although the lettering was a rather formal script, the quality of the lines within the forms and the flow of the text were very fluid and soothing. I wanted Dearest to embody these qualities in order to yield a flowing text, giving the illusion of actual handwriting. Individual characters were selected to serve as the basis for each glyph; they were scanned and significantly altered from the source characters. However, the characteristics of the lines were not convincing enough, so I decided to individually distress each glyph manually (rather than run a distortion filter so often done in "grunge" type) to achieve the desired effect. From here, I wanted to loosen the formality of the script, so many of the angles throughout the font were altered by softening curves and exaggerating some specific features. To make the font more versatile for designers, alternate characters were added to give words the ability to embody a more random, handwritten quality. Finally, add-on swashes were created to allow designers to accentuate the beginning and ending of words and to add emphasis wherever desired. The achieved result is a font unlike any other. I am rather pleased with the finished product.

TF
P22 DEAREST

FD
P22 TYPE FOUNDRY, INC.

TD
CHRISTINA TORRE
BUFFALO NY

January 24, 1836

Dearest Gwendoline,

I cannot keep myself from writing any longer, although I have not had any response to either of my letters. How can I assure you that you have not been out of my thoughts even for one minute since I left you Sunday? You must know how effortlessly I love you & how much I would sacrifice if it were necessary to be married to live ever after with you.

Yours Lovingly,
Michael Hampshire

$$\text{Rialto}^{\text{df}} + \frac{\text{Globetrotter}}{(\text{Azuza} + \text{Keester})} +$$

$$x \frac{\text{Alphatier}}{\text{Dreamer DD}} -$$

```
(Tf) (Typeface Name)
(Fd) (Foundry)
(Db) (Distributor)
(Yr) (Year of Design or Release)
(Cl) (Client)
(Td) (Typeface Designer)
(Fa) (Members of Typeface Family/system)
```

$$\left(\frac{\text{LTR Federal}}{\text{ITC Jeepers}}\right) \times \text{Siemens} + \left(\frac{\text{Mediacore 3}}{\text{Woodley Park}}\right)$$

$$\left(\frac{\text{Dearest - Pradell}}{\text{Whitman - Brioso}}\right) = \underline{\text{15 TDC2 2002 Winners}}$$

TF
RIALTO^{df}

FD
dfTYPE AND KARNER
& STEFAN DEG

TD
GIOVANNI DE FACCIO
VENICE ITALY
LUI KARNER
TEXING AUSTRIA

FA
TITLING
ROMAN
ITALIC
SMALL CAPS
PICCOLO ROMAN
PICCOLO ITALIC
PICCOLO SMALL CAPS
BOLD ROMAN
BOLD ITALIC
BOLD SMALL CAPS

RIALTO^{df}

ABCDEFGHIJKLM
NOPQRSTUVWXYZ
ABCDEFGHIJKLM
NOPQRSTUVWXYZ
abcdefghijklmn
opqrstuvwxyz
1234567890
abcdefgghijklmn
opqrstuvwxyz

TF
WOODLEY PARK

FD
AGFA MONOTYPE

TD
NICK CURTIS
GAITHERSBURG MD

TF
ITC JEEPERS

FD
INTERNATIONAL TYPEFACE
CORPORATION

TD
NICK CURTIS
GAITHERSBURG MD

TF
SIEMENS

CL
SIEMENS

TD
HANS-JÜRG HUNZIKER
PARIS FRANCE

FA
SERIF
SANS
SLAB

Corporate Typeface   **SIEMENS**

Siemens Serif

abcdefghijklmnopqrstuvwxyz1234567890ABCDEFGHIJKLMNOPQRSTUVWXYZ,;!?

abcdefghijklmnopqrstuvwxyz1234567890ABCDEFGHIJKLMNOPQRSTUVWXYZ,;!?

abcdefghijklmnopqrstuvwxyz1234567890ABCDEFGHIJKLMNOPQRSTUVWXYZ,;!?

abcdefghijklmnopqrstuvwxyz1234567890ABCDEFGHIJKLMNOPQRSTUVWXYZ,;!?

abcdefghijklmnopqrstuvwxyz1234567890ABCDEFGHIJKLMNOPQRSTUVWXYZ,;!?

abcdefghijklmnopqrstuvwxyz1234567890ABCDEFGHIJKLMNOPQRSTUVWXYZ,;!?

Siemens Sans

abcdefghijklmnopqrstuvwxyz1234567890ABCDEFGHIJKLMNOPQRSTUVWXYZ,;!?

abcdefghijklmnopqrstuvwxyz1234567890ABCDEFGHIJKLMNOPQRSTUVWXYZ,;!?

abcdefghijklmnopqrstuvwxyz1234567890ABCDEFGHIJKLMNOPQRSTUVWXYZ,;!?

abcdefghijklmnopqrstuvwxyz1234567890ABCDEFGHIJKLMNOPQRSTUVWXYZ,;!?

abcdefghijklmnopqrstuvwxyz1234567890ABCDEFGHIJKLMNOPQRSTUVWXYZ,;!?

abcdefghijklmnopqrstuvwxyz1234567890ABCDEFGHIJKLMNOPQRSTUVWXYZ,;!?

Siemens Slab

abcdefghijklmnopqrstuvwxyz1234567890ABCDEFGHIJKLMNOPQRSTUVWXYZ,;!?

abcdefghijklmnopqrstuvwxyz1234567890ABCDEFGHIJKLMNOPQRSTUVWXYZ,;!?

abcdefghijklmnopqrstuvwxyz1234567890ABCDEFGHIJKLMNOPQRSTUVWXYZ,;!?

abcdefghijklmnopqrstuvwxyz1234567890ABCDEFGHIJKLMNOPQRSTUVWXYZ,;!?

abcdefghijklmnopqrstuvwxyz1234567890ABCDEFGHIJKLMNOPQRSTUVWXYZ,;!?

abcdefghijklmnopqrstuvwxyz1234567890ABCDEFGHIJKLMNOPQRSTUVWXYZ,;!?

TF
GLOBETROTTER

CL
THE STAR GROUP

TD
JAMES LEBBAD
TITUSVILLE NJ

Here comes the sun, do do do do
here comes the sun,

and I say it's all right

Little darling, it's been a long cold lonely winter

Little darling, it feels like years since it's been here

Here comes the sun, do do do do
here comes the sun

and I say it's all right

Little darling, the smiles returning to the faces

Little darling, it seems like years since it's been here

Here comes the sun, do do do do
here comes the sun

and I say it's all right

Sun, Sun, Sun, here it comes...

Little darling, I feel that ice is slowly melting

Little darling, it seems like years since it's been clear

Here comes the sun, do do do do
and I say it's all right

It's all right

In Memory of George Harrison

TF
DREAMER DD

FD
DREAMER DESIGN

TD
ROBIN SPEHAR
TOPANGA CA

FA
PLAIN
ITALIC
BOLD ITALIC
EXTRA BOLD ITALIC
DRUNK

DREAMER DD

DREAMER DD-PLAIN

AABBCCDDEEFFGGHHIIJJKKLLMMN
NOOPPQQRRSSTTUUVVWWXXYYZZ
/0123456789\'""'`'()[]<>->-=.,:;...--
¿¡@#$%&*+=÷†•®©™|`´¥¢£_~^?!

DREAMER DD-ITALIC

AABBCCDDEEFFGG...0123456789?!

DREAMER DD-BOLDITALIC

AABBCCDDEEFFGG...0123456789?!

DREAMER DD-EXTRABOLDITALIC

AABBCCDDEEFFGG...0123456789?!

DREAMER DD-DRUNK

AⱯAB8BCƆCDⱭDEƎEFꟻF...0123456789?!

HIGH ON THE TOP FLOOR OF A TALL, ROUND HOME WORKS A GENIUS.

THIS IS NO ORDINARY BRILLIANT MAN. NO.

PIKE SQUIBBLY IS HIS NAME. DECADES OF HAND LETTERING HAS CONDITIONED HIS MIND, BODY AND SPIRIT. YOU SEE, FOR THE PAST 47 YEARS PIKE HAS BEEN TRANSCRIBING ALL THE LAND'S MOST TREASURED TEXTS. OVER THESE MANY YEARS THE INK HE USES (AN INVENTION OF HIS COUSIN) HAS SEEPED BENEATH HIS FINGERTIPS AND DRIVEN HIM QUITE MAD.

NOW I DO BELIEVE THAT IF I MIX ONE PART "QUICK BROWN FOX"-- TWO PARTS "JUMPS OVER THE LAZY DOG..."

UHH, NO, WAIT A MINUTE... OF COURSE! I'M ON THE WRONG PAGE.... HERE WE ARE-- PAGE 1,258,693...

SUB-SECTION B-74. YES HERE IT IS. "BEGIN BY WHIPPING ONE BEAN-SIZED SPHINX OF BLACK QUARTZ TO A FINE FROTHY FOAM..." HMM-- JUDGING BY THE VOW I TOOK JUST FIVE DAYS AGO, I SHOULD HAVE AT LEAST FIFTEEN BLACK QUARTZ SPHINXES.

NOW WHERE HAVE I PUT THEM?!

?!

OH, BLAST. BLAST. BLAST! BLAST! BLAAAST!!

-:GASP:-

OUCH!

AOUOOH... I FEEL A BIT WOOSY. NO. MORE KINDA OOGY. #%&@! HUF! BLASTED SPHINX OF BLACK QUARTZ! -:MMNN:- GETS ME EVERY TIME...

TF
MEDIACORE

CL
COREMEDIA AG

TD
HEINRICH PARAVICINI
JENS-UWE MEYER
AXEL DOMKE
HAMBURG GERMANY

FA
THIN
LIGHT
REGULAR
CHARACTERS

mⁱMEDIACORE TYPEFACE

↘ FOR **CORPORATE IDENTITY** AND **GRAPHICAL USER INTERFACE**

↘ MEDIACORE **CHAR:**   ABCDEFGHIJKLMNOPQRSTUVWXYZ 1234567890

↘ MEDIACORE **LIGHT:**   ABCDEFGHIJKLMNOPQRSTUVWXYZ 1234567890

↘ MEDIACORE **THIN:**   ABCDEFGHIJKLMNOPQRSTUVWXYZ 1234567890

↘ MEDIACORE **SYMBOL:**

INFO-RESOURCE	WWW	PASTE
USER-MANAGER	UMTS	WAP
DISAPPROVE	TREE	PUBLISH
NEW_DOCUMENT	EXPLORE	GROUP
RENAME	CUT	UNDELETE
CHECKIN	PUBLISH-PREVIEW	SERVER
UNCHECKOUT	APPROVE	QUERY
DESTROY	XML-PREVIEW	DELETE
BACKUP	XSL-TEMPLATE	USER
COPY	SAVE	TREE-OPEN
PRINT_PDF	PREVIEW	...

TF
KEESTER

FD
THE CHANK COMPANY

TD
JIM PARKINSON
OAKLAND CA

KEESTER

ABCDEFGH
IJKLMNOPQ
RSTUVWXYZ
&EFMNW

WHILE WAXING
PARQUET DECKS,
SUEZ SAILORS VOMIT
JAUNTILY ABAFT

TF
LTR FEDERAL

FD
LETTERROR TYPE
& TYPOGRAPHY

TD
ERIK VAN BLOKLAND
THE HAGUE
THE NETHERLANDS

FA
FOUR OPTICAL SIZES
VARIOUS SHADINGS

TF
AZUZA

DB
MY FONTS AND PHIL'S FONTS

TD
JIM PARKINSON
OAKLAND CA

FA
MEDIUM
MEDIUM ITALIC
BOLD
BOLD ITALIC

AZUZA

Medium
ABCDEFGH
IJKLMNOPQRSTU
VWXYZ&
abcdefghijklmno
pqrstuvwxyz

Medium Italic
ABCDEFGH
IJKLMNOPQRSTU
VWXYZ&
abcdefghijklmno
pqrstuvwxyz

Bold
ABCDEFGH
IJKLMNOPQRSTU
VWXYZ&
abcdefghijklmno
pqrstuvwxyz

Bold Italic
ABCDEFGH
IJKLMNOPQRSTU
VWXYZ&
abcdefghijklmno
pqrstuvwxyz

*People who love ideas must have
a love of words, and that means, given a
chance, they will take a vivid interest
in the clothes which words wear.*

— Beatrice Warde

TF
ALPHATIER

TD
MARK JAMRA
PORTLAND ME

FA
LIGHT
MEDIUM
BOLD

Alphatier

It does genuinely matter that a designer should take trouble and take delight in his choice of typefaces. The trouble and delight are taken not merely "for art's sake" but for the sake of something so subtly and intimately connected with all that is human that it can be described by no other phrase than "the humanities." If "the tone of voice" of a typeface does not count, then nothing counts that distinguishes man from the other animals. ...there is reality in the imponderable, and that not only notation but connotation is part of the proper study of mankind. The best part of typographic wisdom lies in this study of connotation, the suitability of form to content.

¶ A specimen (see S. Morison, 'Byzantine Elements in Humanist Script' illustrated from the "Aulus Gellius" of 1445, "Special Paper of the Wesmorale Library"), from a foundry in New York, printed in 1820, has taken particular notice of "The Philadelphia Foundry."

C'est dans la salle à manger

Grüße aus Bad Oldesloe

A 25% change in height

Carpe Diem ▶(Latin)

TDC2 2001
ERRATA

CA
TYPEFACE

TF
PEPE

TD
PEPE GIMENO
GODELLA SPAIN

FA
REGULAR
ALTERNATE

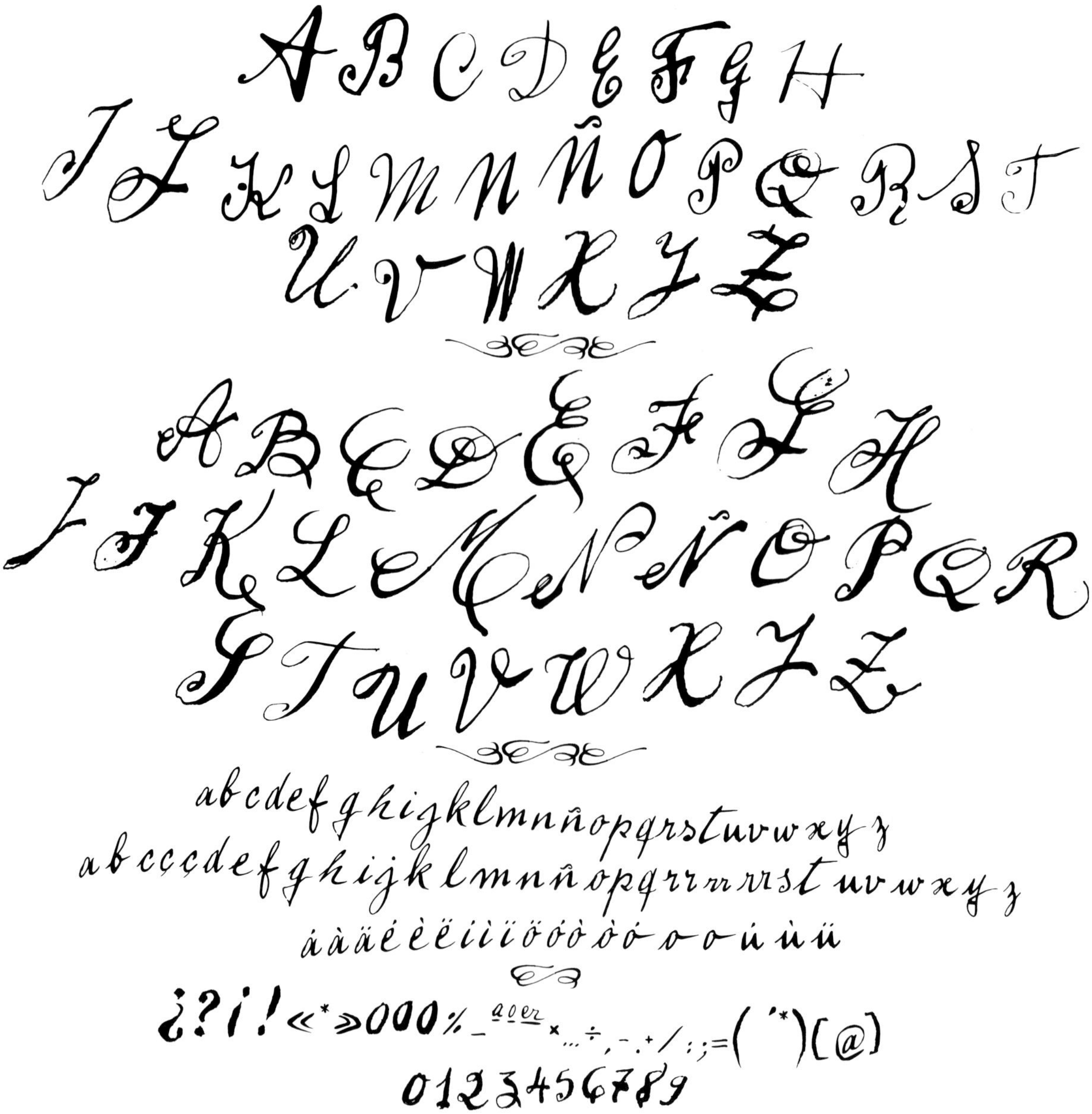

TDC 47
ERRATA

CA
LOGOTYPE

DS
ADI STERN
TEL AVIV ISRAEL

CL
BATSHEVA DANCE COMPANY

DE
ADI STERN

AD
ADI STERN

CD
ADI STERN

TY
HANDMADE

ALEX W. WHITE
TDC DIRECTOR-AT-LARGE

WHAT DO TDC **48** AND TYPOGRAPHY **23** MEAN?

The Type Directors Club (TDC) was founded in 1946 during a postwar expansion of advertising in America. The type director was responsible for all typography and typesetting that came out of an ad agency, and the art director had not yet risen to equal partnership with the copywriter in creative development.

Ed Gottschall, president of the TDC in 1967 and 1968, wrote in 1971's TDC 25th Anniversary keepsake booklet, "(Beginning in 1943) a few men in New York who took type very seriously used to get together for lunch (at Schraffts and the Brass Rail) and talk about advertising typography…. The Type Directors Club was formed in October 1946."

The TDC began a lecture series in 1947 that, for the next ten years, grew into an institution. Topics included the development of the printed word, type textures in design, individualism in typography, type and direct advertising, wood engraving and type, type in publications, and typography in advertising.

In 1954 the TDC's annual lecture series concluded with a show of typography. This was the first Type Directors Club Show. It had fifty samples.

As the lectures were fazed out — the topics had been adopted by local schools, many taught by TDC members — the Show continued and grew. There were 100 winners in 1957 and 200 winners in 1958. By comparison, this 2002 TDC annual contains 156 winners selected from 2,350 submissions from 32 countries.

Catalogs of the TDC Typography Show were printed in *Art Direction* magazine. In 1979 the TDC catalog became a book. This evolution was marked by a new name: *Typography 1*. We are now at *Typography 23*. Samples of the TDC's Show catalogs from 1954 to 1979 are rare. Only a few complete sets are known to exist. They contain 4,149 winners culled from 50,650 entries.

Here is a brief selection of winners shown in the TDC catalogs the year they won. Though they have become design icons, their publication in the TDC Show catalogs was the first time these samples received professional recognition.

Since 1946 the Type Directors Club has recognized the very best typography in the world. It is irresistible to consider which of the winners in this annual might join the ranks of the immortal.

1954

FIRST
TDC SHOW

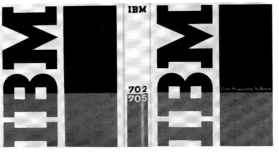

1956

BOB
GILL

ALEXY
BRODOVITCH

1957 CHAIRMAN
TOBIAS MOSS

1957 JUDGES
GEORGE KRIKORIAN
AARON BURNS
LEO LIONNI
WILL BURTIN
HERB LUBALIN
ALVIN EISENMAN
PAUL RAND
GENE FEDERICO
LADISLAV SUTNAR
ALLEN HURLBURT
BRADBURY THOMPSON

1957

PAUL
RAND

1958

WILL
BURTIN

LADISLAV
SUTNAR

1959

BRADBURY
THOMPSON

1960

LESTER
BEALL &
RICHARD
ROGERS

OTTO
STORCH &
WILLIAM
CADGE

1961

HENRY
WOLF

1962

MALCOLM
MANSFIELD

GEORGE
KLAUBER

1963

BERT
STEINHAUSER

1964

BEN
ROSEN

1967

CARL
DAIR

1968

MILTON
GLASER

1969

DIETMAR R.
WINKLER

HERB
LUBALIN

1970

TOM
CARNASE

1974

BILL
BONNELL III

1975

ALAN
PECKOLICK

1976

GERARD
HUERTA

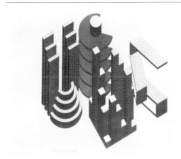

1977

TAKENOBU
IGARASHI

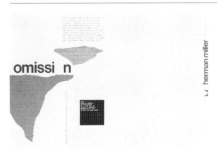

1978

JOHN
MASSEY

1979

HERB
LUBALIN

UNA® AARO 2002 S	DONA® ABUAF 2001 S	MARCELLE® ACCARDI 1998 S	CHRISTIAN® ACKER 2002 S	ERIC® ALB 1996 ∷	NATASCHA® AMPUNANT 2002 S	GAIL® ANDERSON 2002 ∷	JACK® ANDERSON 1996 ∷	DEBI® ANI 2001 ∷	MARTYN® ANSTICE 1992 ∷	MAGNUS® ARASON 2000 ∷
DON® ARIEV 1998 ∷	PAMELA® ARNOLD 2001 ∷	PHILIPP® ARNOLD 2000 ∷	GERARD® BABAKIAN 2001 ∷	ROBERTO® BAGATTI 2001 ∷	JAQUES® BAGIOS 1995 ∷	PETER® BAIN 1986 ∷	CHRISTINE® BAJAK 2001 ∷	BORIS® BALANT 1999 ∷	MARCO® BALECKE 2000 ∷	BRUCE® BALKIN 1993 ∷
STEPHEN® BANHAM 1995 ∷	NEIL® BARNETT 2001 ∷	STEVE® BARRETTO 2002 ∷	DAVID® BARRINEAU 1996 S	BARBARA® BAUMANN 1996 ∷	GERD® BAUMANN 1995 ∷	CLARENCE® BAYLIS 1974 ∷	CHRIS® BEAN 2000 ∷	SYNDI® BECKER 1996 ∷	FELIX® BELTRAN 1988 ∷	ED® BENGUIAT 1964 ∷
ANNA® BERKENBUSCH 1989 ∷	RONALD® BERNARD 2002 ∷	JOHN® BERRY 1996 ∷	PETER® BERTOLAMI 1969 ∷	DAVIDE® BEVILACQUA 1999 ∷	TAD® BIERNOT 2000 ∷	KLAUS® BIETZ 1993 ∷	CHRISTINA® BIJAK 2002 ∷	HENRIK® BIRKVIG 1996 ∷	ROGER® BLACK 1980 ∷	SARA® BLAKELY 2002 S
MARC® BLAUSTEIN 2001 ∷	ANTHONY® BLOCH 2002 ∷	CLAAS® BLÜHER 2001 S	ALAN® BOARTS 1996 ∷	KARLHEINZ® BOELLING 2086 ∷	SARA® BONNAFANT 2002 S	GIANNI® BORTOLOTTI 2098 ∷	STEPHEN® BOSS 2002 ∷	THAD® BOSS 2001 ∷	JAMIE® BOYLE 1999 S	PATRICIA® BRADBURY 1993 ∷
FRED® BRADY 1997 ∷	KEVIN® BRAINARD 2002 ∷	BUD® BRAMAN 1990 ∷	STEVEN® BRAWER 2002 ∷	ED® BRODSKY 1980 ∷	PETER® BRUHN 2000 ∷	ANDREAS® BRUNLINGHAUS 1997 ∷	STEFAN® BUCHER 2002 ∷	BILL® BUNDZAK 1964 ∷	STEVE® BYERS 1998 ∷	PATRICIA® BYRNES 2001 ∷
ANDREW® BYROM 2002 ∷	BILL® CAHAN 2002 ∷	RONN® CAMPISI 1988 ∷	SCOTT® CARSLAKE 2001 ∷	MATTHEW® CARTER 1988 ∷	SERGIO® CASTRO 2001 ∷	TONY® CASUSCELLI 2002 ∷	KEN® CATO 1988 ∷	PAUL® CAULLETTT 1998 S	HENRIQUE® CAYATTE 2001 ∷	JOOYEON® CHAE 2001 S
CINDY® CHAN 2002 S	ERIC® CHAN 1997 ∷	LESLIE® CHAN 2001 ∷	THESEUS® CHAN 1994 ∷	VIRGINIA® CHAN 2000 S	KAI PING® CHAO 2001 ∷	LEN® CHEESEMAN 1993 ∷	JEFF® CHEN 2002 S	DAVID® CHEUNG, JR. 1998 ∷	HEUNG®- HEUNG CHIN 1998 ∷	KATHRYN® CHO 2002 S

★ CHARTER MEMBER ◊ HONORARY MEMBER S STUDENT MEMBER A ASSOCIATE MEMBER

KAI-YAN® CHOI 1990 ••

TSWEI® CHUANG-WAI 2002 ••

STANLEY® CHURCH 1997 ••

TRACI® CHURCHILL 1995 ••

JOHN V.® CLARKE 1999 ••

TRAVIS® CLIETT 1953 ••

GRAHAM® CLIFFORD 1998 ••

TOM® COCOZZA 1976 ••

LISA® COHEN 1993 ••

STUART® COHEN 1996 ••

DIANNE® COLE 2001 S

ANGELO® COLELLA 1990 ••

REMIE® COLESTOCK 2000 S

ED® COLKER 1983 ••

DAVID® COOKE 2001 ••

NICK® COOKE 2001 ••

RODRIGO® CORRAL 2002 ••

MADELEINE® CORSON 1996 ••

SUSAN® COTLER-BLOCK 1989 ••

FREEMAN® CRAW 1947 ★

JUAN JOSE® GIMENO CRESPO 2001

LAURA® CROOKSTON 2000 ••

BART® CROSBY 1995 ••

RAY® CRUZ 1999 ••

JEFF® CULVER 1997 S

DAVID® CUNDY 1985 ••

BRIAN® CUNNINGHAM 1996 ••

RICK® CUSICK 1989 ••

MICHAEL® DAMARE 1998 ••

TIMEA® DANCS 2001 S

SUSAN® DARBYSHIRE 1987 ••

KAREN® DAVIDSON 2001 ••

BILL® DAWSON 2001 ••

EINAT LISA® DAY 1997 S

JESUS DE® FRANCISCO 2001 S

JOSANNE DE® NATALE 1986 ••

MATEJ® DECKO 1993 ••

RICHARD® DENDY 2000 ••

MARGI® DENTON 1999 ••

MARK® DENTON 2001 ••

W. BRIAN® DIECKS 1998 ••

CLAUDE A.® DIETERICH 1984 ••

KIRSTEN® DIETZ 2000 ••

JOSEPH® DIGIOIA 1996 ••

KRISTINA® DIMATTEO 2002 ••

TONY® DIPIETRO 2001 ••

NIKOLA® DJUREK 2002 ••

TOM® DOLLE 1995 ••

LOU® DORFSMAN 1954 ••

GONZALO® PEREYRA DOVAL 2002 S

PASCALE® DOVIC 1997 ••

STEPHEN® DOYLE 1998 ••

JOHN® DREYFUS 1968 ◊

CHRISTOPHER® DUBBER 1985 ••

MARTIN® DUFFY 2002 ••

JEFFERY L.® DUNAJ 2001 ••

SIMON® DWELLY 1998 ••

LUTZ® DZIARNOWSKI 1992 ••

LASKO® DZUROVSKI 2000 ••

BRIAN® EDLEFSON 2001 ••

FRIEDRICH® EISENMENGER 1993 ••

DR. ELSI® VASSDAL ELLIS 1993 ••

GARRY® EMERY 1993 ••

STEFAN® ENGELHARDT 2001 ••

HC® ERICSON 2001 ••

NICK® ERICSON 2001 ••

FABIENNE® ERNI 2001 S

BETTINA® ERTL 2002 ••

RAFAEL® ESQUER 2000 ••

JOSEPH® MICHAEL ESSEX 1978 ••

LESLIE® EVANS 1992 ••

FLORENCE® EVERETT 1989 ••

DANIEL® EWER 2000 ••

PETER® FAHRNI 1993 ••

JOHN® FAIRLEY 2000 ••

SIMON® FAIRWEATHER 2001 ••

JOHN R.® FALKER 2000 ••

DAVID® FAREY 1993 ••

MICHAEL® FARMER 1994 ••

SEAN® FERMOYLE 2000 ••

ANTERO® FERREIRA 1997 ••

SIMON® FITTON 1994 ••

KRISTINE® FITZGERALD 1990 ••

ROBERT® FLECK 2001 ••

GONÇALO® FONSECA 1993 ••

WAYNE® FORD 1996 ••

CARIN® FORTIN 2002 ••

THOMAS® FOWLER 1993 ••

ALESSANDRO®
FRANCHINI
1996
::

HENRIK-JAN®
FRANCKE
2001
::

ARTUR®
FRANKOWSKI
2000
::

CAROL®
FREED
1987
::

HUGH WERNER
FREITAS®
2000
S

TOBIAS®
FRERE-JONES
2000
::

SAAR®
FRIEDMAN
2002
::

BAERBEL®
FRITZ
2001
::

ADRIAN®
FRUTIGER
1967
◊

MARIO®
FUHR
1997
::

TEIJI®
FUJII
2001
::

SARAH®
GAGER
2002
S

LOUIS®
GAGNON
2002
::

OHSUGI®
GAKU
2001
::

MARCELO®
GARCIA
2002
S

CHRISTOF®
GASSNER
1990
::

MARTINA®
GATES
1996
S

DAVID®
GATTI
1981
::

GEMMA®
GATTI
2001
S

MATTHEW®
GAYNOR
2000
S

FRANK®
GERMANO
2001
::

ROBYN®
GILL-ATTAWAY
1993
::

LOU®
GLASSHEIM
1947
★

HOWARD®
GLENER
1977
::

GIULIANO®
CESAR
GONÇALVES
2001

HOLLY®
GOSCINSKY
1998
S

EDWARD®
GOTTSCHALL
1952
::

NORMAN®
GRABER
1969
::

DIANA®
GRAHAM
1985
::

AUSTIN®
GRANDJEAN
1959
::

EWAN®
GREEN
2002
::

STEPHEN®
GREEN
1997
::

KAREN®
GREENBERG
1995
::

AGNES LAYGO
GREGORIO®
2001
::

SIMON®
GRENDENE
2002
S

JAMES®
GRIESHABER
1996
::

AMELIA®
GROHMAN
2002
S

FRANK E.E.®
GRUBICH
1996
::

ROSANNE®
GUARARRA
1992
::

IVAN®
GUARINI
2001
::

CHRISTIANE®
GUDE
1997
::

OLGA®
GUTIERREZ DE
LA ROZA
1995

EINAR®
GYLFASON
1995
::

PETER®
GYLLAN
1997
::

TOMI®
HAAPARANTA
2001
::

WILLIAM®
HAFEMAN
1996
::

ALLAN®
HALEY
1978
::

CRYSTAL®
HALL
1997
::

DEBRA®
HALL
1996
::

SONJA®
HALLER
2002
S

RYAN®
HALVERSON
2002
S

ANGELICA®
HAMANN
2001
S

GARRICK®
HAMM
2001
::

YOUNG-HEE®
HAN
2002
S

VICTORIA®
HANES
2002
S

EGIL®
HARALDSEN
2000
::

KEITH®
HARRIS
1998
::

KNUT®
HARTMANN
1985
::

BONNIE®
HAZELTON
1975
::

AMY®
HECHT
2001
::

ERIC®
HEIMAN
2002
::

ARNE®
HEINE
2000
::

FRANK®
HEINE
1996
::

EARL M.®
HERRICK
1996
::

KLAUS®
HESSE
1995
::

KATHY®
HETTINGA
2001
::

ERIC®
HEUPEL
2000
S

FONS M.®
HICKMANN
1996
::

JAY®
HIGGINS
1988
::

ELISE®
HILPERT
2000
::

HELMUT®
HIMMLER
1996
::

NORIHIKO®
HIRATA
1996
::

CHARLES®
HIVELY
2001
::

J. DREW®
HODGES
1995
::

MICHAEL®
HODGSON
1989
::

JONATHAN®
HOEFLER
2000
::

BARBARA®
HOFFAR
2001
S

JULIA®
HOFFMANN
2002
S

FRITZ®
HOFRICHTER
1980
::

ROMAN®
HOLT
1999
::

SHANNON®
HOLT
2001
::

CHRISTY®
HONG
2001
S

KEVIN®
HORVATH
1987
::

FABIAN®
HOTZ
2001
::

DIANA®
HRISINKO
2001
::

JAMES®
HUANG
2001
S

ANTON®
HUBER
2001
::

SANDRA®
HUDSON
2002
::

* CHARTER MEMBER ◊ HONORARY MEMBER S STUDENT MEMBER A ASSOCIATE MEMBER

| EVA® HUECKMANN 2001 S | DAVID® HUKARI 1995 :: | HYUN-JU® HWANG 2002 S | MIRKO® ILIĆ 2002 :: | ANTHONY® INCIONG 2002 :: | YANEK® IONTEF 2000 :: | ELIZABETH® IRWIN 2000 :: | TERRY® IRWIN 1996 :: | MITSUO® ISHIDA 2002 :: | DONALD® JACKSON 1978 ◊ | ED® JACOBUS 2001 :: |

| ANGELA® JAEGER 2002 :: | MICHAEL® JAGER 1994 :: | MARK® JAMRA 1999 :: | SILAS® JANNSEN 2001 :: | JOANNE® JAWOROWSKI 2002 :: | DAVID R.® JENNINGS 2001 :: | DAVID® KADAVY 2002 S | OTSO® KALLINEN 2000 S | JOHN® KALLIO 1996 :: | I-CHING® KAO 2002 S | MIE® KASHIWAGI 2001 S |

| DITI® KATONA 2002 :: | DOROTHEA® KAUMANNS 2002 S | TOYOSHIMA® KAYA 2002 S | NAN® KEETON 1997 :: | BRUNNETTE® KENAN 1999 :: | KAY® KHOO 1999 :: | JANG HOON® KIM 1997 :: | JUNE HYUNG® KIM 2000 S | YEUNKYUM® KIM 2000 S | BO-RAM® KIM 2001 S | SOO® KIM 2002 S |

| RICK® KING 1993 :: | PAUL® KINGETT 2000 :: | KATSUHIRO® KINOSHITA 2002 :: | RHINNAN® KITH 2001 S | THEO® KLOOSTER 2001 :: | SAMUEL® KNIGHT 2001 :: | NANA® KOBAYASHI 1994 :: | AKIRA® KOBAYASHI 1999 :: | CLAUS® KOCH 1996 :: | BORIS® KOCHAN 2002 :: | MASAYOSHI® KODAIRA 2002 :: |

| JESSE TAYLOR KOECHLING® 1998 S | JESSICA® KOMAN 2001 :: | STEVE® KOPEC 1974 :: | ANDERS® KORNESTEDT 2002 :: | MARCUS® KRAUS 1997 :: | MATTHIAS® KRAUS 2002 :: | AVI® KRAVITZ 2001 S | STEPHANIE® KREBER 2001 :: | BERNHARD J. KRESS® 1963 :: | WALTER® KRYSHAK 2000 :: | TOSHIYUKI® KUDO 2000 :: |

| FELIX® KUNKLER 2001 :: | CHRISTIAN® KUNNERT 1997 :: | DOMINIK® KYECK 2002 :: | GERRY® L'ORANGE 1991 :: | RAYMOND F. LACCETTI® 1987 :: | PATRICIA® LACHMAN 2002 S | REGINA® LAMBERTI 2001 S | MELCHIOR® LAMY 2001 :: | JOHN® LANGDON 1993 :: | GUENTER® GERHARD LANGE 1983 | JEAN® LARCHER 2001 :: |

| MARCIA® LAUSEN 2001 :: | DAVID® LAWTER 2001 :: | JAMES® LEBBAD 2001 :: | GUY® LEBLANC 2002 :: | CHRISTINE® LEE 2002 S | JAE® LEE 2001 :: | SARA® LEE 2002 S | SUSANA® LEE 2001 S | DAVID® LEMON 1995 :: | RANDI DAVIS® LEVIN 2001 :: | OLAF® LEU 1965 :: |

| ADAM® LEVITE 1997 :: | RENEE® LEVITT 1998 S | OPAS® LIMPI-ANGKANAN 2002 | KIM® LINCOLN 2002 :: | JAN® LINDQUIST 2001 :: | MILES MARKUM LINKLATER® 1998 :: | CHRISTINE® LINNEHAN 2001 :: | MONICA® LITTLE 1998 :: | WALLY® LITTMAN 1960 :: | ESTHER® LIU 1998 :: | UWE® LOESCH 1996 :: |

| BENG YEW® LOH 2001 S | JOHN HOWLAND LORD® 1947 ◊ | ARLINE® LOWE 2001 :: | ALEXANDER® LUCKOW 1994 :: | FRANK® LUEDICKE 1999 :: | GREGG® LUKASIEWICZ 1990 :: | LINNEA® LUNDQUIST 1999 :: | FRANK® LYNCH 2001 :: | MATT® LYNCH 2001 :: | MICHAEL® MACNEILL 2002 :: | DANUSCH® MAHMOUDI 2001 :: |

| HEIDI® MAKINO 2001 S | DIDIER® MALCHAIRE 2002 :: | OHSUGI® MANBU 2001 :: | CHAD® MARCHESE 2001 S | MARILYN® MARCUS 1979 :: | MARIE® MARIUCCI 1998 :: | JULIE® MARKFIELD 2001 :: | LINDSEY® MARSHALL 2001 :: | KERRY® MARTIN 2002 :: | IGOR® MASNJAK 1998 :: | TED® MAUSETH 2001 :: |

| ANDREAS® MAXBAUER 1995 :: | EILEEN® MCCARREN 2000 S | ROD® MCDONALD 1995 :: | CAMERON® MCFATRIDGE 2002 S | MARK® MCGARRY 2002 :: | PATRICIA® MCGILLIS 2002 :: | JOHN® MCGREW 2001 :: | BARBARA® MCKENZIE 2001 :: | MARC A.® MEADOWS 1996 :: | DONNA® MEADOWS MANIER 2000 :: | GABRIEL® MARTINEZ MEAVE 2001 :: |

| MATEVZ® MEDJA 2002 :: | ROLAND® MEHLER 1992 :: | UWE® MELICHAR 2000 :: | DR. FRIEDER® MELLINGHOFF 1999 :: | JEFF® MERRELLS 1999 :: | FRÉDÉRIC® METZ 1985 :: | DAVID® MICHAELIDES 1997 :: | TONY® MIKOLAJCZYK 1997 :: | BRIAN® MILLER 2001 :: | JENNIFER® MILLER 2001 :: | JOE® MILLER 2002 :: |

| JOHN® MILLIGAN 1978 :: | ELENA® MIRANDA 2001 :: | MICHAEL® MIRANDA 1984 :: | RALF® MISCHNICK 1998 S | DEAN® MITCHELL 2000 :: | SUSAN L.® MITCHELL 1996 :: | BERND® MOELLENSTAEDT 2001 :: | MICHAEL® MOESSLANG 1999 :: | PREETI® MONGA 2002 :: | SAKOL® MONGKOLKASE-TARIN 1995 S | JAMES® MONTALBANO 1993 :: |

| CHRISTINE® MOOG 1999 S | RICHARD EARL MOORE® 1982 :: | MINORU® MORITA 1975 :: | JOHN MICHAEL MORRIS® 1998 :: | LARS® MÜLLER 1997 :: | JOACHIM® MÜLLER-LANCÉ 1995 :: | GARY® MUNCH 1997 :: | MATTHEW® MUNOZ 2002 S | JERRY KING® MUSSER 1988 :: | ALEXANDER® MUSSON 1993 :: | LOUIS A.® MUSTO 1965 :: |

| CRISTIANA® NERI-DOWNEY 1997 :: | HELMUT® NESS 1999 :: | ROBERT® NEWMAN 1996 :: | DAVID® NG 2000 :: | LILLIAN® NG 2000 S | THU® NGUYEN 2002 :: | BONNIE® NICOLAS 2001 S | RAYMOND® NICHOLS 2001 :: | MARIA® NICKLIN 2001 :: | CHARLES® NIX 2000 :: | SHUICHI® NOGAMI 1997 :: |

| GERTRUD® NOLTE 2001 S | ALEXA® NOSAL 1987 :: | JACK® ODETTE 1977 :: | HOLGER® OEHRLICH 2002 :: | NINA V.® OERTZEN 1999 :: | TSKAAKI® OKADA 2002 S | AKIO® OKUMARA 1996 :: | MICHEL® OLIVIER 1994 :: | ERIK® OLSEN 2001 :: | OISIN® O'MALLEY 1998 S | KEVIN® O'NEILL 2002 :: |

ROBERT®
OVERHOLTZER
1994
∷

MICHAEL®
PACEY
2001
∷

NORMAN®
PAEGE
1999
∷

FRANK®
PAGANUCCI
1985
∷

ENRIQUE®
PARDO
1999
∷

SHARON MEE
SUN PARK®
2001
S

JIM®
PARKINSON
1994
∷

LYNDI®
PARRETT
2001
S

GUY®
PASK
1997
∷

KIM®
PAULSEN
2001
∷

GUDRUN®
PAWELKE
1996
∷

ADAM ROBERT
PEELE®
2001
S

DANIEL®
PELAVIN
1992
∷

ROBERT®
PETERS
1986
∷

OANH®
PHAM-PHU
1996
∷

KEN®
PHILLIPS
1999
∷

MAX®
PHILLIPS
2000
∷

CLIVE®
PIERCY
1996
∷

IAN®
PILBEAM
1999
∷

MARGARET®
PISCITELLI
2000
S

ALBERT-JAN®
POOL
2000
∷

NEIL®
POWELL
2001
∷

WILL®
POWERS
1989
∷

RANDAL®
PRESSON
2001
∷

VITTORIO®
PRINA
1988
∷

JAMES®
PROPP
1997
∷

JOCHEN®
RAEDEKER
2000
∷

ERWIN®
RAITH
1967
∷

RENEE®
RAMSEY-
PASSMORE
1999

SAL®
RANDAZZO
2000
∷

MATTHEW®
RASCOFF
2001
S

NIKKI®
RASHEED
2001
∷

BOB®
RAUCHMAN
1997
∷

MARGARET®
RE
2002
∷

JO ANNE®
REDWOOD
1988
∷

PAUL®
REED
2000
S

HANS DIETER
REICHERT®
1992
∷

CRYSTAL®
REID
2001
∷

KASEY®
REIS
2002
S

LIZ®
REITMAN
1997
∷

HEATHER L.®
REITZE
2001
∷

FABIAN®
RICHTER
2001
∷

ROBERT®
RINDLER
1995
∷

PHILLIP®
RITZENBERG
1997
∷

JOSE®
RIVERA
2001
∷

RICK®
ROAT
1999
∷

NADINE®
ROBBINS
1995

CHAD®
ROBERTS
2001
S

PHOEBE®
ROBINSON
2002
S

FRANK®
ROCHELL
1999
∷

SALVADOR®
ROMERO
1994
∷

EDWARD®
RONDTHALER
1947
*

KURT®
ROSCOE
1993
∷

ZVIKA®
ROSENBERG
2002
∷

GABRIELA®
ROTARU
2000
S

DELRAE®
ROTH
2001
∷

JOSEPH®
RUIZ
2001
∷

PAUL®
RUSTAND
1999
∷

ERKKI®
RUUHINEN
1986
∷

TIMOTHY J.®
RYAN
1996
∷

CAROL-ANNE®
RYCE-PAUL
2001
S

MICHAEL®
RYLANDER
1993
∷

GREG®
SADOWSKI
2001
∷

GUS®
SAELENS
1950
∷

ILJA®
SALLACZ
1999
∷

DAVID®
SALTMAN
1966
∷

INA®
SALTZ
1996
∷

RODRIGO®
SANCHEZ
1996
∷

ALEJANDRA®
SANTOS
2001
S

STEPHANIE®
SASSOLA-
STRUSE
1997

NATHAN®
SAVAGE
2001
∷

JOHN®
SAYLES
1995
∷

DAVID®
SAYLOR
1996
∷

HARTMUT®
SCHAAR-
SCHMIDT
2001

MATTHIAS®
SCHÄFER
1997
S

HANS DIRK®
SCHELLNACK
2001
∷

MARTIN®
SCHITTO
2001
∷

THOMAS®
SCHLANGE
2002
∷

PETER®
SCHLIEF
2000
S

HERMANN J.®
SCHLIEPER
1987
∷

HOLGER®
SCHMIDHUBER
1999
∷

HERMANN®
SCHMIDT
1983
∷

KLAUS®
SCHMIDT
1959
∷

MARKUS®
SCHMIDT
1993
∷

CHRISTIAN®
MARC SCHMIDT
2002
S

BERTRAM®
SCHMIDT-
FRIDERICHS
1989

WERNER®
SCHNEIDER
1987
∷

EILEEN HEDY®
SCHULTZ
1985
∷

| ECKEHART® SCHUMACHER -GEBLER 1985 | APRIL® SCOTT 2001 S | JO® SCRABA 1997 S | MATHEW® SEARCY 2001 S | JAMES® SEEGERT 2002 | ENRICO® SEMPI 1997 | JESSICA® SHATAN 1995 | MARK E.® SHAW 1999 | PAUL® SHAW 1987 | PHILIP® SHORE, JR. 1992 | ERIC® SHROPSHIRE 2001 |

| ROBERT® SIEGMUND 2001 S | LORINDA® SIEGRIST 2002 S | MARK® SIMKINS 199 2 | CHRISTOPHER SIMMONS® 2002 | SCOTT® SIMMONS 1994 | ARABA® SIMPSON 2002 S | MAE® SKIDMORE 1998 | FINN® SKÖDT 2000 | MARTHA RICE SKOGEN® 1999 | PAT® SLOAN 1997 | BILL® SMITH 2001 |

| SILVESTRE® SEGARRA SOLER 1995 | MARTIN® SOLOMON 1955 | JAN® SOLPERA 1985 | RONNIE TAN® SOO CHYE 1988 | BRIAN® SOOY 1998 | GEOVANY® SOSA 2002 S | ERIK® SPIEKERMANN 1988 | VICTOR® SPINDLER 2001 | DENISE® SPIRITO 2002 | FRANK® STAHLBERG 2000 | ROLF® STAUDT 1984 |

| THOMAS® STECKO 1994 | LEE® STEELE 2000 | OLAF® STEIN 1996 | CHARLES® STEWART 1992 | CHARLES® STONE 2001 | PAIGE® STONHAUS 2002 | WILLIAM® STREEVER 1950 | ILENE® STRIZVER 1988 | KATJA® STUKE 1997 | HANSJORG® STULLE 1987 | NEIL® SUMMEROUR 2002 |

| DEREK® SUSSNER 2001 | TRACEY® SUTHERLAND 2002 S | ZEMPAKU® SUZUKI 1992 | JOANNA® SWANSON 2002 | CAROLINE® SZETO 2002 S | LAURIE® SZUJEWSKA 1995 | KAN® TAI-KEUNG 1997 | DOUGLAS® TAIT 1998 | YUKICHI® TAKADA 1995 | YOSHIMARU® TAKAHASHI 1996 | MILACK® TALIA 2001 S |

| KAREN® TANAKA 2001 | JACK® TAUSS 1975 | PAT® TAYLOR 1985 | ANTHONY J.® TEANO 1962 | JOHANN® TERRETTAZ 2002 | RÉGINE® THIENHAUS 1996 | TERRIE® THOMPSON 2002 | WAYNE® TIDSWELL 1996 | ROBERT® TIDWELL 2002 | ERIC® TILLEY 1995 | COLIN® TILLYER 1997 |

| MARTIN KO® TIN-YAU 2001 | LAURA® TOLKOW 1996 | GIORGIO® TRAMONTINI 2001 | JEAN-MARC® TROADEC 2001 S | KLAUS® TROMMER 1999 | NIKLAUS® TROXLER 2000 | MINAO® TSUKADA 2000 | VIVIANE® TUBIANA 2001 | MARC® TULKE 2000 | JAMES® TUNG 1997 | FRANÇOIS® TURCOTTE 1999 |

| MICHAEL® TUTINO 1996 | CAROLINE® ULRICH 2001 | JANET® UPEGUI 2001 S | MATTHEW® URZUA 2001 S | DIEGO® VAINESMAN 1991 | PATRICK® VALLEÉ 1999 | CHRISTINE® VAN BREE 1998 | KEVIN® VAN DER LEEK 1997 | JAN VAN DER® PLOEG 1952 | RYAN® VAN METER 1999 | MICHELLE® VAN SANTEN 2001 |

★ CHARTER MEMBER   ◊ HONORARY MEMBER   S STUDENT MEMBER   A ASSOCIATE MEMBER

JANINE® VANGOOL 2001 ••

YURI® VARGAS 1999 ••

ANNA® VILLANO 1999 S

ANNETTE® VON BRANDIS 1996 ••

THILO® VON DEBSCHITZ 1995 ••

ALEX® VOSS 1998 ••

FRANK® WAGNER 1994 ••

OLIVER® WAGNER 2001 ••

ALLAN R.® WAHLER 1998 ••

JUREK® WAJDOWICZ 1980 ••

SERGIO® WAKSMAN 1996 ••

GARTH® WALKER •• 1992

STEPHAN® WALTER •• 2001

XU® WANG 1993 ••

JANE® WARD 1998 S

EMILY® WARDWELL 2001 S

KATSUNORI® WATANABE 2002 ••

ALYCE® WAXMAN 2001 S

JANET® WEBB 1991 ••

HARALD® WEBER 1999 ••

MATT® WEBER 1998 ••

JOY® WEEENG 1993 S

KURT® WEIDEMANN 1966 ••

CLAUS F.® WEIDMUELLER 1997 ••

SYLVIA® WEIMER 2001 ••

ELIZABETH® WELSH 2001 ••

JUSTIN® WENDEL 2001 S

MARCO® WENZEL 2002 ••

JUDY® WERT 1996 A

ALEX® WHITE 1993 ••

ALBERT L.® WHITLEY, JR. 1998 S

ALEX® WIGINGTON 2001 ••

HEINZ® WILD 1996 ••

RICHARD® WILDE 1993 ••

JAMES® WILLIAMS 1988 ••

JOSEPH R.® WILLIAMS 1998 S

CONNIE® WILSON 2002 ••

GRANT® WINDRIDGE 2000 ••

CAROL® WINER 1994 ••

CONNY J.® WINTER 1985 ••

DELVE® WITHRINGTON 1997 ••

DAISY® WONG 2001 ••

PETER C.® WONG 1996 ••

ANUTHIN® WONGSUNKA-KON 1998 S

FRED® WOODWARD 1995 ••

LAURA COE® WRIGHT 1999 ••

CHIEN HUI® YANG 2000 S

RONALD® YEUNG 2000 ••

JUN® YONEYAMA 2002 S

SOPHIA® YOON 2001 S

CHENG® YU-PIN 2001 ••

HERMANN® ZAPF 1952 ◊

DAVID® ZAUHAR 2001 ••

STEPHEN® ZHANG 2001 ••

MAXIM® ZHUKOV 1996 ••

ROY® ZUCCA 1969 ••

JEFF® ZWERNER 1997 ••

SUSTAINING MEMBERS 2002 ••

LITTLE BROWN & COMPANY 2002 ••

PENTAGRAM DESIGN, INC. SAN FRANCISCO 2002 ••

MEMBERSHIP AS OF APRIL 30, 2002 ••

TYPE DIRECTORS CLUB
60 EAST 42ND STREET
SUITE 721
NEW YORK, NY 10165
PHONE 212-983-6042
FAX 212-983-6043
E-MAIL
DIRECTOR@TDC.ORG
WEB SITE WWW.TDC.ORG

FOR MEMBERSHIP
INFORMATION PLEASE
CONTACT THE TDC OFFICE.

BOARD OF DIRECTORS
2001/2002

OFFICERS

PRESIDENT
DANIEL PELAVIN

VICE PRESIDENT
JAMES MONTALBANO
(TERMINAL DESIGN, INC.)

SECRETARY/TREASURER
GARY MUNCH
(MUNCHFONTS)

DIRECTORS-AT-LARGE
JOHN D. BERRY
STEVE BYERS
RONN CAMPISI
(RONN CAMPISI DESIGN)
MATTHEW CARTER
(CARTER & CONE)
BRIAN DIECKS
(THE DIECKS GROUP, INC.)
CHARLES NIX
(CHARLES NIX &
ASSOCIATES)
ALEX WHITE (AW DESIGN)
CAROL WINER (HADASSAH)

EXECUTIVE DIRECTOR
CAROL WAHLER

BOARD OF DIRECTORS
2002/2003

OFFICERS

PRESIDENT
JAMES MONTALBANO,
(TERMINAL DESIGN, INC.)

VICE PRESIDENT
GARY MUNCH
(MUNCHFONTS)

SECRETARY/TREASURER
ALEX WHITE (AWVC)

DIRECTORS-AT-LARGE
JOHN D. BERRY
BRIAN DIECKS
(THE DIECKS GROUP, INC.)
NANA KOBAYASHI
(FOOTE CONE BELDING)
SUSAN L. MITCHELL
(FARRAR STRAUS & GIROUX)
CHARLES NIX
(CHARLES NIX &
ASSOCIATES)
DIEGO VAINESMAN
(MJM CREATIVE SERVICES)
CAROL WINER (HADASSAH)

CHAIRMAN OF THE BOARD
DANIEL PELAVIN

EXECUTIVE DIRECTOR
CAROL WAHLER

COMMITTEE FOR
TDC48/TDC2 2002

CHAIRPERSONS
KLAUS SCHMIDT
GARY MUNCH

DESIGNER
DESIGN:MW

CO-COORDINATORS
CAROL WAHLER
KLAUS SCHMIDT

ASSISTANTS TO JUDGES
ABIGAIL ARAFELI
CELY FAIRWEATHER
SIMON FAIRWEATHER
NATHALIE B. KIRSHEH
NANA KOBAYASHI,
ROSEMARY MARKOWSKY
SUSAN MCCARTY
JAMES MONTALBANO
OMAR MRVA
DANIEL PELAVIN
ADAM S. WAHLER
ALLAN R. WAHLER
MATTHEW WEBER

TDC PRESIDENTS
FRANK POWERS, 1946, 1947
MILTON ZUDECK, 1948
ALFRED DICKMAN, 1949
JOSEPH WEILER, 1950
JAMES SECREST,
1951, 1952, 1953
GUSTAVE SAELENS,
1954, 1955
ARTHUR LEE, 1956, 1957
MARTIN CONNELL, 1958
JAMES SECREST, 1959, 1960
FRANK POWERS, 1961, 1962
MILTON ZUDECK, 1963, 1964
GENE ETTENBERG, 1965, 1966
EDWARD GOTTSCHALL,
1967, 1968
SAADYAH MAXIMON, 1969
LOUIS LEPIS, 1970, 1971
GERARD O'NEILL, 1972, 1973
ZOLTAN KISS, 1974, 1975
ROY ZUCCA, 1976, 1977
WILLIAM STREEVER, 1978,1979
BONNIE HAZELTON, 1980,1981
JACK GEORGE TAUSS, 1982,
1983
KLAUS F. SCHMIDT, 1984, 1985
JOHN LUKE, 1986, 1987
JACK ODETTE, 1988, 1989
ED BENGUIAT, 1990, 1991
ALLAN HALEY, 1992, 1993
B. MARTIN PEDERSEN,
1994, 1995
MARA KURTZ, 1996, 1997
MARK SOLSBURG, 1998,1999
DANIEL PELAVIN 2000, 2001

TDC MEDAL RECIPIENTS
HERMANN ZAPF, 1967
R. HUNTER MIDDLETON, 1968
FRANK POWERS, 1971
DR. ROBERT LESLIE, 1972
EDWARD RONDTHALER, 1975
ARNOLD BANK, 1979
GEORG TRUMP, 1982
PAUL STANDARD, 1983
HERB LUBALIN, 1984
(POSTHUMOUSLY)
PAUL RAND, 1984
AARON BURNS, 1985
BRADBURY THOMPSON,
1986
ADRIAN FRUTIGER, 1987
FREEMAN CRAW, 1988
ED BENGUIAT, 1989
GENE FEDERICO, 1991
LOU DORFSMAN, 1995
MATTHEW CARTER, 1997
ROLLING STONE MAGAZINE,
1997
COLIN BRIGNALL, 2000
GÜNTER GERHARD LANGE,
2000

SPECIAL CITATIONS
TO TDC MEMBERS
EDWARD GOTTSCHALL, 1955
FREEMAN CRAW, 1968
JAMES SECREST, 1974
OLAF LEU, 1984, 1990
WILLIAM STREEVER, 1984
KLAUS F. SCHMIDT, 1985
JOHN LUKE, 1987
JACK ODETTE, 1989

2002 SCHOLARSHIP
RECIPIENTS
LORRAIN ABRAHAM
(PRATT INSTITUTE)
GRACE CHOU
(THE COOPER UNION)
ANNA DJAHOVA
(MARYLAND INSTITUTE
COLLEGE OF ART)
JULIANA FAJARDO
(FASHION INSTITUTE OF
TECHNOLOGY)
TANAPORN MAY JAMPATHOM
(PARSONS SCHOOL
OF DESIGN)
NATSUMI NISHIZUMI
(SCHOOL OF VISUAL ARTS)
VERA EVSTAFIEVA
(MOSCOW STATE UNIVERSITY
OF PRINTING ARTS)

INTERNATIONAL LIAISON
CHAIRPERSONS

ENGLAND
DAVID FAREY
HOUSESTYLE
50-54 CLERKENWELL ROAD
LONDON EC1M 5PS

FRANCE
CHRISTOPHER DUBBER
SIGNUM ART
94, AVENUE VICTOR HUGO
94100 SAINT MAUR DES
FOSSES

GERMANY
BERTRAM SCHMIDT-
FRIDERICHS
VERLAG HERMANN SCHMIDT
MAINZ GMBH & CO.
ROBERT KOCH STRASSE 8
POSTFACH 42 07 28
55129 MAINZ HECHTSHEIM

JAPAN
ZEMPAKU SUZUKI
JAPAN TYPOGRAPHY
ASSOCIATION
SANUKIN BLDG. 5 FL.
1-7-10 NIHONBASHI-HONCHO
CHUO-KU, TOYKO 104-0041

MEXICO
PROF. FELIX BELTRAN
APARTADO DE CORREOS
M 10733 MEXICO 06000

SWITZERLAND
ERIC ALB
SYNDOR PRESS
P. O. BOX 5334
CH 6330 CHAM

VIETNAM
RICHARD MOORE
21 BOND STREET
NEW YORK, NY 10012